around **PARIS** with **KIDS**

by Jennifer Ditsler-Ladonne
and Emily Emerson Le Moing
4th EDITION
FODOR'S TRAVEL PUBLICATIONS
New York ✳ Toronto ✳ London ✳ Sydney ✳ Auckland
www.fodors.com

CREDITS
Writers: Jennifer Ditsler-Ladonne and Emily Emerson Le Moing

Editor: Caroline Trefler
Editorial Production: Carrie Parker
Production Manager: Steve Slawsky

Design: Fabrizio La Rocca, *creative director*; Tigist Getachew, *art director*
Illustration and Series Design: Rico Lins, Keren Ora Admoni/Rico Lins Studio

ABOUT THE WRITERS

After nearly 20 years in Manhattan, writer and editor Jennifer Ditsler-Ladonne married a Frenchman, moved to Paris, and became a mother, all in one year. Now, with her husband and five-year-old daughter, Inès, she is busily (and very happily) discovering the many joys of being a parent in Paris.

Emily Emerson Le Moing is an American writer who moved to France for a year in 1979 and can't seem to leave. These days she divides her time between Paris, Montreal, and her ramshackle 15th-century farmhouse in the Loire Valley.

Fodor's Around Paris with Kids

Fourth Edition
ISBN 978-1-4000-0516-1
ISSN 1533-5313

An Important Tip and an Invitation

Although all prices, opening times, and other details in this book are based on information supplied to us at press time, changes occur all the time in the travel world, and Fodor's cannot accept responsibility for facts that become outdated or for inadvertent errors or omissions. So always confirm information when it matters, especially if you're making a detour to visit a specific place. Your experiences—positive and negative—matter to us. If we have missed or misstated something, please write to us. We follow up on all suggestions. Contact the Around Paris with Kids editor at editors@fodors.com or c/o Fodor's at 1745 Broadway, New York, NY 10019.

Special Sales

This book is available at special discounts for bulk purchases for sales promotions or premiums. Special editions, including personalized covers, excerpts of existing guides, and corporate imprints, can be created in large quantities for special needs. For more information, write to Special Markets/Premium Sales, 1745 Broadway, New York, NY 10019 or e-mail specialmarkets@randomhouse.com.

PRINTED IN THE UNITED STATES OF AMERICA
10 9 8 7 6 5 4 3 2 1

COUNTDOWN TO GOOD TIMES

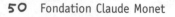

GET READY, GET SET!

Paris may be the world's most romantic capital, but it's also a wonderful city to visit with kids, even if you don't speak French. In this book you'll find 68 ways for parents and children to spend a terrific couple of hours, or an entire day, whether your family loves culture, history, or just seeing the sights. While some destinations are meant mostly for kids, there are not many must-see places in Paris that don't cater to children: meaning that there's almost always something for everyone. For families who want a more in-depth experience, we've listed dozens of workshops for children and parents who want to rub elbows with their French counterparts while learning something new. Almost anywhere you go in Paris, you'll find pretty little parks with play areas, tasty snacks, and kid-friendly attractions, because this sophisticated city has made a big effort to develop a wealth of educational and fun activities for young Parisians and visitors.

My advice is to head first for the Tour Eiffel, hands-down the city's top sight for most kids, and then relax in the Jardin du Luxembourg, a very Parisian park with all sorts of areas to play or relax. Another big hit, especially at night, is a ride on one of the *bateaux mouches* tour boats that cruise the Seine. Use the neighborhood directory (All Around Town) and the thematic directory (Something for Everyone) at the back of this book to help make your plans. Whatever you do, make sure to avoid museum overload and take the time to sit back and relax in a park, munch a baguette, and appreciate this beautiful city.

SAVING MONEY

Only regular adult and kids' prices are listed; children under the ages specified are free. Always ask whether any discounts are offered for a particular status or affiliation (bring your ID). Many attractions sell family tickets or long-term memberships. Some places—mostly museums and other cultural destinations—are always free to anyone under 18 and to everyone one day a month (usually the first Sunday) or one evening a week.

The invaluable Paris Museum Pass (available at participating museums, monuments, tourist offices, métro stations, and FNAC stores; see www.parismuseumpass.com) gets you into more than 60 local museums and monuments at a discount and often without standing in line (the time-saving feature is sometimes the most important if your kids, like many, get cranky when waiting in line); two-day (€32), four-day (€48), or six-day (€64) cards are available. The pass is for people 18 and over; almost all the attractions it covers are free for those under 18. You can also purchase special transportation-plus-admission tickets for many attractions just outside Paris, from the SNCF (the national rail company) at train stations or SNCF offices.

The Passe Navigo, with unlimited métro and bus travel for a week or a month, can be a big money-saver; choose your card by the number of zones. A two-zone card covers central Paris and the near suburbs, and kids' cards are available at a discount. If you're planning a shorter stay, the Paris-Visite card, sold at all métro and train stations, gives unlimited travel on area métros, trains, trams, and buses for one to five days; passes for kids 4–11 are half price, children under four ride free. For central Paris only, choose the card for zones 1–3; for Paris airports or Disneyland Paris, choose the card for zones 1–5. This card also grants discounts to a number of attractions. Ever more métro stations in Paris are fully automated but don't be daunted by the ticketing machines; they're in English, simple to use, and take credit cards. For more information on public transport, see the Paris transit authority's Web site, www.ratp.fr, and click on the British flag for English.

EATING OUT

Paris restaurants are generally more expensive than their U.S. counterparts but most offer kids' menus or will prepare a special kids' meal on request. Yes, you can find hamburgers and steaks (specify *bien cuit,* for well done; or *à point,* for medium) if you don't want them served rare, and *frites* (french fries), but French-style fast food is more likely to consist of crêpes (look for street-corner stands everywhere), *croque monsieur* sandwiches (grilled ham and cheese), baguette sandwiches, and open-face sandwiches (*tartines*). High-quality chains—two to look for are Paul and Cojean—are proliferating throughout the city, where anything from fresh salads, quiche, gourmet sandwiches, and French-style desserts can be enjoyed at the table or taken out. Other quality on-the-go options can be picked up at *traiteurs* (traditional shops selling takeout prepared food) and *pâtisseries* (pastry shops). Picnickers should note that most city parks don't let you sit on the grass (though it's fine to do so in the city's *bois,* or woods). Do what the French do, and have your picnic on a park bench.

Many Paris restaurants close in August, and most close at least one day a week, usually Sunday (especially at night) and/or Monday. Call ahead to make sure a restaurant will be open and to make reservations. Lunch is generally served from 12 to 2, and the evening meal begins at around 7:30 at the earliest. Tearooms, brasseries, and cafés tend to be open during the day, though tearooms usually close in the evening. Café prices for a coffee and croissant are cheaper if you stand at the counter rather than sit at a table. Now that smoking has been prohibited in all indoor spaces, there is no need to worry about the smoky cafés and restaurants of old.

GETTING AROUND
Paris is divided into 20 arrondissements (administrative districts) that spiral out from the center like a snail's shell, starting with the first. Each arrondissement has its own character and its own *mairie* (city hall). Arrondissements are listed in this book in the French manner (e.g., 6e is the 6th arrondissement), following addresses.

Traffic is heavy throughout Paris, sidewalks are small and crowded, and people drive really fast, so be especially careful crossing streets; many drivers run red lights. Scooters and even motorcycles often take shortcuts on sidewalks. On the métro, watch for the gap between platforms and cars and be careful of sliding doors, they can give a real pinch to big and little fingers. Always hold children's hands when boarding and exiting.

The Paris métro system is fast, efficient, economical, easy to use, and generally safe, although you should avoid empty cars at night and watch out for skilled pickpockets; the métro closes at around 1 AM and at 2 AM on Friday and Saturday. One ticket per person lets you ride as far as you like within central Paris. Kids' tickets are discounted. A 10-ticket *carnet* is more economical than buying separate tickets; a Paris Visite card (*see* Saving Money, *above*) is the best choice if you're planning a short stay; for a week or longer the Passe Navigo is your best bet. The RER system (suburban commuter trains, such as the ones that run to the two Paris airports) requires separate RER tickets, available from ticket booths in RER and métro stations, but be sure to hold on to your ticket, unlike the métro, you'll need it to exit the RER station. Paris buses are fun for kids, but the routes are sometimes difficult to follow. (Pick up a "Paris Bus" brochure at any métro station or check the maps posted at bus stops.) You can pay with a métro ticket or cash, but each time you change buses, you must pay again. Paris's new Tram 3 is a sleek tramway that runs along the city's southern edge; pay with a métro ticket.

For older kids who can handle a full-size bike, Paris's Vélib' bicycles are a great way to get around for those undaunted by city traffic. Vélib' stands can easily be found in every neighborhood and take all major credit cards. A one-day pass costs ⇐1 and a seven-day pass is ⇐7. Although Paris drivers are used to sharing the road with cyclists, and there are now many designated bicycle lanes, be sure to read up on laws and safety tips beforehand on the Vélib' Web site (www.velib.paris.fr), as cycling laws are strictly enforced.

WHEN TO GO

With the exception of seasonal attractions, kid-oriented destinations are generally busiest when children are out of school—especially weekends, Wednesdays (when many French schools either organize field trips or have no classes), holidays (especially two-week school vacations, generally in early November, at Christmas, in early March, and at Easter), and July and August. Most sights are less crowded at meal times (generally, 1–2 and 7–9). Some attractions are closed when schools are closed, but others add extra hours on these days. Check ahead if you plan to visit an attraction on a holiday.

RESOURCES AND INFORMATION

If you have special interests or want to find out about events scheduled during your visit, contact the Office de Tourisme de la Ville de Paris (25-27 rue des Pyramides, tel. 08-92-68-30-00, www.parisinfo.com) or the Espace du Tourisme d'Île de France (Carrousel du Louvre underground shopping mall, 99 rue de Rivoli, tel. 08-26-16-66-66). The Web site of the Mairie de Paris (www.paris.fr) is another good source.

For information (in French) on weekly events, try *Pariscope* (www.pariscope.fr), *Le Monde* (www.lemonde.fr), and *Libération* (www.liberation.fr), available at newsstands. *Paris-Mômes* (www.parismomes.fr) and *Citizen Kid* (www.paris.citizenkid.com) are excellent online guides to events just for kids. If your children would like to practice French on a French Web site for kids, try www.momes.net. To get online, you'll find Internet cafés in every Paris neighborhood, and most hotels have Internet connections. Wi-Fi (wireless) connections are widely available, including in many parks and gardens.

FINAL THOUGHTS

Taking one of the many classes for kids and families that are offered by Paris's museums and cultural centers is a great way to interact with Parisians and learn something about the city, too, even if you don't speak French. Most instructors speak at least some English (as do most Parisians), so you'll be with people who share your interests, and your kids may make some French friends.

Lots of moms and dads were interviewed to create these suggestions, and we'd love to add yours. E-mail us at editors@fodors.com (specify Around Paris with Kids on the subject line), or write to us at Fodor's Around Paris with Kids, 1745 Broadway, New York, NY 10019. In the meantime, bon voyage!

—Jennifer Ditsler-Ladonne

AQUABOULEVARD

Paris may be in northern Europe, but you'd never know it once you step into this water-lovers' wonderland. A year-round indoor-outdoor water park, Aquaboulevard lets you take a trip to the tropics without leaving the heart of the city. In summer, Aquaboulevard's outdoor beach and pool area, open June–August, is one of the city's most popular sunbathing spots.

Feel like basking on the sand? You can, year-round, on the artificial beach surrounding the outdoor pool. Want to bodysurf? The waves won't please experienced surfers, but small kids enjoy jumping them. Tired of sidewalks, buildings, and traffic noise? The landscape here surrounds you with tropical vegetation and the sounds of flowing water. You can also swim through fountains, get splashed by waterfalls, wade in a river, and—most popular among kids—careen through tunnels and down 11 long slides that end with a splash into a pool. (Different age groups have different slides.) Parents aching from too much

KEEP IN MIND You could combine your visit here with a visit to the Parc Georges Brassens (see #10) by taking a ride on Paris's newest electric tramway, the T3, which runs along the southern edge of the city and stops near the Balard métro stop. Like other trams Paris has put into service, the T3 is designed to help reduce the city's crippling traffic and pollution problems. The T3's ultramodern cars swish almost silently along on rails lined with grass, giving you a close-up view of the work of several international artists whose sculptures are displayed along the way. Leave it to Paris to make even its tram routes chic. Buy an individual ticket or use your Paris-Visite pass.

4–6 rue Louis-Armand,
15e. Métro: Pl.-Balard

 €25 ages 12 and up, €12
children 3–11; admission
is for 6 hrs

 M–Th and Su 9 AM–11 PM,
F 9 AM–12 PM, Sa 8 AM–midnight

01-40-60-10-00; www.
aquaboulevard.com

 3 and up

sightseeing can enjoy a sauna or relax in bubbling hot tubs, and though kids might not need the tubs' therapeutic benefits, they do like the bubbles.

A star attraction here is the life-size model of a whale commissioned by Jacques Cousteau, the late French explorer and film personality who did so much to increase awareness of aquatic environments throughout the world. Because all 27 meters (90 feet) of Madame Whale is hollow, kids can crawl inside and get a close-up look at a whale's inner workings. A gentle slide leading out into a pool is the preferred exit, even for the smallest kids. Children who favor dry land have a special play area where they don't even have to get wet. All in all, the complex is one of the city's best antidotes to stress.

MAKE THE MOST OF YOUR TIME

Aquaboulevard can get extremely crowded. To avoid the crush in July and August, try to come during mealtimes (12–2 or 7–9). Note that baggy shorts–type bathing suits for men and boys are not allowed; brief-style swimwear is required.

EATS FOR KIDS There are eight food outlets within Aquaboulevard, though lines get long at lunchtime. Next door is a branch of family-friendly **Hippopotamus** (4 rue Louis-Armand, tel. 01–53–98–91–20) with tables overlooking Aquaboulevard's pools. **Le Bistrot d'André** (232 rue St-Charles, tel. 01–45–57–89–14) serves French home cooking; try the roast leg of lamb. For a splurge, visit the **River Café** (146 quai de Stalingrad, Issy-les-Moulineaux, tel. 01–40–93–50–20), about a half-mile away. This barge on the Seine is a trendy but friendly restaurant. For food see also Parc André Citroën (#13).

ARC DE TRIOMPHE

One of the world's best-known memorials to military might, this massive monument dates from the early 19th century but its construction was as up-and-down as the fortunes of the man who had it built.

The Arc de Triomphe (Arch of Triumph) was commissioned by Napoléon in 1806 to commemorate his victory at the Battle of Austerlitz. Little more than the foundations had been finished by 1810, when Napoléon married, so a wood-and-canvas mock arch was erected for the celebrations. When Napoléon lost at Waterloo in 1815, construction was put on hold. The monument was finally finished in 1836, in time for Napoléon's coffin (he had died in 1821) to be hauled through it in a grandiose procession in 1840. Today, the arch is the site of France's Tomb of the Unknown Soldier, where a flame has been kept burning since 1923; it's rekindled every evening at 6:30.

MAKE THE MOST OF YOUR TIME To check out the carvings on the outside of the arch (representing—what else?—war scenes), you'll need to be on the sidewalks on the outer edges of the place Charles-de-Gaulle. The carving entitled *Le Départ des Volontaires* (Departure of the Volunteers) is considered the best.

EATS FOR KIDS **Alléosse** (13 rue Poncelet, tel. 01–46–22–50–45) is a cheese store on a lively food-market street. **Maison Pou** (16 av. des Ternes, tel. 01–43–80–19–24) has served delicious charcuterie since 1830, before the arch was finished. **Dragons Élysées** (11 rue de Berri, tel. 01–42–89–85–10) has a wide choice of Chinese dishes, but the main attraction for kids is the giant aquarium under your feet, thanks to a glass floor; reserve in advance for a table above the aquarium. **La Maison du Chocolat** (225 rue du Faubourg-St-Honoré, tel. 01–42–27–39–44) has some of the best chocolate in Paris. For food see also Palais de la Découverte (#14) and École Lenôtre (#51).

Pl. Charles-de-Gaulle, 8e.
Métro: Charles-de-Gaulle-Étoile

 €9 adults 18 and up

 Apr–Sept, daily 10 AM–11 PM;
Oct–Mar, daily 10 AM–10:30 PM

01-55-37-73-77

8 and up

As far as kids are concerned, the most interesting thing about the Arc de Triomphe isn't its history but the view from the top: 45 meters (148 feet) above the place Charles-de-Gaulle (formerly the place de l'Étoile and still called that by Parisians). You can take an elevator, but most children prefer to climb the stairs, all 284 of them. Halfway up, a little museum shows a film on the monument's history. From the rooftop terrace you can check out the 12 streets that radiate like a star out from the square: note avenue Foch, Paris's widest street. You'll see that Paris is bisected by a broad paved line leading straight from the Arc du Carrousel, in front of the Louvre, through the Arc de Triomphe all the way to the Grande Arche in the western suburb of La Défense, with the Champs-Élysées to the east of the arch and the avenue de la Grande Armée to the west. You'll also get a great view of Paris's chaotic traffic swirling nonstop below you.

KEEP IN MIND From atop the Arc, you can really appreciate why most visitors avoid driving in Paris. You'll see vehicles of all kinds whirling around, seemingly randomly, in every direction. For a break from the craziness, stroll down avenue Hoche (northeast of the Arc) to the Parc Monceau, an elegant park with many monuments, a pretty play area and sandbox, plenty of benches, and some grassy spots where you can sit for a discreet picnic lunch; the park was painted by Claude Monet in 1878.

ARÈNES DE LUTÈCE

Take a trip back in time to the days before Paris was Paris—to the 1st through 3rd centuries AD, when this was a bustling Gallo-Roman stronghold called Lutetia, population 6,000. Hidden away behind apartment buildings in the Left Bank district, just off bustling rue Monge, is a city park with a remnant of that time: the Arènes de Lutèce (Lutetia Arena).

Built into a hillside, the arena was used for circus and theatrical productions until around AD 280, when invading barbarians destroyed it and most other Gallo-Roman structures on the Left Bank. For 1,600 years the arena was forgotten, but then at the end of the 19th century its ruins were unearthed during the construction of a line of the Paris métro nearby. The arena's first use after rediscovery, however, was as a parking lot for buses.

Today the Arènes de Lutèce has been excavated and refurbished, but only to the extent that its stonework is now solid and secure. The city wisely chose not to make the ancient structure into a museum, but rather to give it new life as a public park, and the plan worked:

EATS FOR KIDS Pick up some goodies and picnic with Parisians on the arena's stone steps. A popular open-air market on the place Monge operates Wednesday, Friday, and Sunday mornings, while the nearby rue Mouffetard has scores of food shops, open Tuesday through Sunday. **Cave La Bourgogne** (144 rue Mouffetard, tel. 01–47–07–82–80), a quintessential French bistro and wine bar, is a neighborhood favorite: daily specials (like sole meunière, charcuterie, or cassoulet) are written on the blackboard and served inside, or on the outdoor terrace. **Le Jardin des Pâtes** (4 rue Lacépède, tel. 01–43–31–50–71) serves organic vegetarian dishes.

Rue des Arènes, 5e.
Métro: Pl. Monge, Cardinal-Lemoine

 08-92-68-30-00 Office de Tourisme;
www.parisinfo.com

 Free

 Daily 8–sunset

All ages

now the arena is one Paris monument that doesn't feel like a monument at all. Locals love to come; tourists rarely seek the place out. Just as thousands of aristocratic Lutetians used to enjoy watching performances here, today's parents enjoy sitting on the stone seats watching their kids play soccer in the arena's sandy ring. Children who don't like soccer can climb around on the steep stone benches.

The north side of the arena has a shady little park called the square Capitan, with a gurgling fountain, a play area with a sandbox and jungle gyms, several benches perfect for a picnic, and the Maison des Oiseaux (House of Birds, tel. 01-55-43-30-45, 6 rue des Arènes, open Saturday 1–6 PM), which has exhibits on the 100 or so species of wild birds that live in Paris.

MAKE THE MOST OF YOUR TIME

Steep stone stairs and walls without guardrails are dangerous for children under 5, particularly toddlers. Smaller children can safely play on the level court in the center of the arena, however, or in the park and play area on the arena's north side.

KEEP IN MIND A tribe of Gauls called the Parisii lived on what's now the Île de la Cité (home to Notre-Dame) from the 3rd century BC to the arrival of the Romans in 52 BC. The Gauls' resistance to Roman rule is spoofed in the popular Astérix comic-book series, which inspired its own theme park (see Parc Astérix, #12). The Romans eventually defeated the Gauls and built their own city, Lutetia, which contained the arena, some public baths, a long aqueduct, and other structures. After the barbarians destroyed Lutetia in AD 280, a group of Gauls rebuilt the city and, in 360, named it Paris, in honor of their ancestors.

BATEAUX PARISIENS

65

Kids can't help but love *bateaux mouches*, the tourist boats that glide up and down the Seine through central Paris. With their big glass roofs and huge spotlights that illuminate the city's monuments at night, they look impossibly garish, but once on board, you'll be rewarded with a spectacularly beautiful view of the city and its graceful bridges seen from the water, a reminder that Paris has been a river port for thousands of years. As for the term *bateaux mouches*, which means "fly boats," it comes from the Les Mouches district of Lyon, where the boats were originally manufactured. Of all the tour-boat operators—and there are many—a sound choice is Bateaux Parisiens, which is particularly good for the younger set.

Regular cruises begin near the Eiffel Tower or Notre-Dame and set off for a one-hour voyage that goes up or down the river under various bridges, including the Passerelle des Arts (the footbridge between the Louvre and the Left Bank), past Notre-Dame, the Louvre, the Eiffel Tower, and the tiny Île des Cygnes (Island of the Swans). Don't miss the replica

EATS FOR KIDS Treat yourself to ice cream at Paris's legendary *glacière* **Berthillon** (31 rue St-Louis-en-Île, tel. 01–43–54–31–61) near Notre-Dame. You can choose from more than 65 delectable flavors. The parlor is closed in August, but the ice creams and sorbets are also available from vendors throughout the Île St. Louis.

MAKE THE MOST OF YOUR TIME Another great choice for cruising the Seine is the **Batobus** (tel. 08–25–05–01–01, www.batobus.com), a leisurely water taxi (with no commentary) that makes stops at eight of Paris's major sites, including the Tour Eiffel, Notre-Dame, Musée d'Orsay, and the Louvre. Like a bus, you can get on or hop off at any of the stops. A day pass costs €13 ages 16 and up, or €7 children 15 and under; two- and five-day passes are available also. To find the stops, look for the little Batobus signs along the quais of the Seine. In general, the boats operate mid-Mar–May and Sept–Oct, daily 10–7; June–Aug, daily 10–9:30; and Nov–mid-Mar, daily 10:30–4:30.

Port de la Bourdonnais, 7e.
Métro: Bir-Hakeim-Grenelle;
Quai Montebello, 4e. Métro: Cité

 from €11 ages 12 and
up, €5 children 3–11;
Croisière Enchantée from €9

Apr–Sept, daily 10 AM–10:30 PM every ½ hr
or hr; Oct–Mar, daily 10–10 every ½ hr or
hr; Croisière Enchantée Oct–May and Sept,
Sa–Su; Jun–Jul, Wed and Sa–Su; daily some
school holidays

08-25-01-01-01 meal reservations;
01-76-64-14-66 Croisière Enchantée;
www.bateauxparisiens.com

All ages; kids'
cruises ages 2–8

of sculptor Frédéric-Auguste Bartholdi's Statue of Liberty on the end of the Île des Cygnes—the real, original statue was built in Paris in 1886. The cruises that begin near the Eiffel Tower are on large boats equipped with free headphones that let you listen to commentary in a choice of 12 languages, while a loudspeaker blares stirring music in the background. The cruises that begin near Notre-Dame are on smaller boats and a guide tells you about what you're seeing, in five different languages. Lunch and dinner cruises with live music give you some of the best dining-room views in Paris, but the meals are not cheap.

A special one-hour Croisière Enchantée (Enchanted Cruise) is geared to kids 2–8 and their parents. A pair of elves (professional actors) entertain by singing songs and telling stories (in French) about the monuments you're sailing past. Where else can you find singing elves on the Seine? Offered daily at 3:45 PM.

KEEP IN MIND Paris is divided into Left Bank (Rive Gauche) and Right Bank (Rive Droite), referring to the banks of the Seine from the point of view of a person sailing downstream (with the current). If your boat is traveling upstream toward Notre-Dame and the narration points out the Musée d'Orsay on the Left Bank, you should actually look to your right. The Louvre, on the Right Bank, will be on your left. Got it? Watch people turn their heads back and forth trying to figure out what's going on.

BERCY VILLAGE

Eastern Paris is on the move, with major developments like Omnisports (the Bercy sports and entertainment complex, www.bercy.fr), a Frank Gehry–designed building that's the new home of the Cinémathèque Française (France's prestigious cinema and the cinema museum, www.cinemathequefrancaise.com), the national library, and now Bercy Village, where a once-scruffy collection of *chais* (wine depots) on the city's eastern edge has been turned into a popular destination for families. You'll find plenty of diversions and room for kids to run around.

These handsome stone structures are historic landmarks, and now house branches of some of Paris's trendiest shops, most of which offer activities for kids on Wednesdays and Saturdays. All cluster around an attractive courtyard, the Cour St-Émilion. Bercy Village also organizes lively treasure hunts for kids 6–11, with clues in French, Wednesday afternoons at 3, Mar.–June, Sept., Oct.

The Bercy Village complex is at the eastern end of the 25-acre Parc de Bercy–Yitzhak Rabin, Paris's newest major park, which contains century-old trees, a pond with curved bridges

KEEP IN MIND If seeing the Seine near Bercy Village gives you the urge to plunge in, don't. Instead, pay a visit to Paris's only floating swimming pool, the Piscine Josephine Baker (quai François-Mauriac, tel. 01–56–61–96–50), across the river from Bercy Village by way of the Passerelle Simone de Beauvoir. The pool—named for the American entertainer who became a big success in France—sits on a floating platform covered with glass panels. There's a wading pool for younger kids, and you'll have great views of the river.

Cour St-Émilion, 12e.
Métro: Cour-St-Émilion

01–40–02–90–80;
www.bercyvillage.com

 Free

Daily 24 hrs

All ages

over it, several kids' play areas, themed gardens that include a kid-friendly labyrinth, and a huge lawn that kids can actually play on. In a gesture to the area's wine-oriented past, there's even a vineyard. The Maison du Jardinage (House of Gardening), near the center of the park, schedules classes in gardening for kids and adults on weekends during the school year or daily in July and August (in French; tel. 01–53–46–19–19).

One of the wine depots is home to Le Musée des Arts Forains (Museum of Circus Arts) and its fascinating collection of circus-related items. Another attraction, anchored just across the Seine from the Parc de Bercy, via the Passerelle Simone de Beauvoir (a footbridge), is Le Cabaret Pirate, an authentic Chinese junk that's been turned into a restaurant, theater, and nightclub; kids' shows are given regularly. On your way to the footbridge, don't miss the statue *21 Enfants du monde*, in which recycled materials depict 21 kids from all over the world. As the French say, *Ça bouge à Bercy* (Bercy is where it's happening).

MAKE THE MOST OF YOUR TIME
Contact Nature et Découvertes (tel. 01–53–33–82–40) for family-oriented nature activities or FNAC Éveil et Jeux (tel. 01–44–73–01–58) for activities related to books and music, and Loisirs et Création (tel. 01–53–17–11–90), a crafts shop that often gives demonstrations. All are on the Cour St-Émilion. The Musée des Arts Forains is open to groups only, but you can request to be part of a group (tel. 01–43–40–16–15).

EATS FOR KIDS All the Bercy Village restaurants on the Cour St-Émilion welcome families. Possibilities include **Compagnie de Crêpes** (tel. 01–43–40–24–40) for savory and dessert crêpes; **Partie de Campagne** (tel. 01–43–40–44–11) for sandwiches, salads, and quiches to take out or eat in; **The Frog at Bercy** (tel. 01–43–40–70–71), a microbrewery and pub; **Hippopotamus** (tel. 01–44–73–88–11), which specializes in grilled meats and fries; and **T pour 2** (tel. 01–40–19–02–09), a tearoom.

BOIS DE BOULOGNE

The vast Bois de Boulogne (Boulogne Woods) was once a wild, dangerous forest where the kings of France hunted wolf, deer, and wild boar. (It's still unwise to venture into its wooded areas at night, although animals aren't the problem these days.) Napoléon III gave the forest to Paris in the mid-19th century, and developer Baron Haussmann, who was carving huge boulevards through the city at the time, laid streets through the woods as well, modeling his plan on London's Hyde Park. Today, the park is popular among Parisians looking for fresh air and open spaces.

At the Lac Inférieur (the larger of the park's two lakes), you can rent paddleboats or bicycles, and at the Lac Supérieur, kids bring remote-controlled boats and buzz them around the lake. The park also contains two race courses: the Hippodrome d'Auteuil (tel. 01–40–71–47–47), which stages steeplechases (with jumps and hurdles) regularly March–December, and the Hippodrome de Longchamp (tel. 01–44–30–75–00), which hosts flat racing April–October. On the first Sunday in October, you can watch top Thoroughbreds compete in the world's richest horse race, the Arc de Triomphe.

KEEP IN MIND Although many of the Bois de Boulogne's attractions are near métro stops, you'll need a car or bicycle to tour the whole park. Bikes can be rented near the entrance to the Jardin d'Acclimatation (see #45) and near the boat ramp at the Lac Inférieur.

MAKE THE MOST OF YOUR TIME If you have any tennis fans in your family, be sure to take a little detour to Tenniseum (2 av. Gordon-Bennett, métro Porte-d'Auteuil, tel. 01–47–43–48–48, www.rolandgarros.com), a museum in honor of one of France's favorite sports, located on Court 3 of Rolland-Garros, the country's most famous tennis complex and the home of the French Open. The museum traces the history of tennis, has video terminals where you can watch historic matches of the past, and offers a guided tour of Rolland-Garros itself for an extra charge.

Main entrances: Porte Maillot, Porte de la Muette,
Porte de Passy, 16e. Métro: Porte d'Auteuil, Porte Dauphine,
Porte de la Muette, Porte de Passy

 08–92–68–30–30 Office de Tourisme;
www.parisinfo.com or www.paris.fr

 Free

 Daily 24 hrs

All ages

The gorgeous Parc de Bagatelle, within the Bois de Boulogne, contains a little château built in 1755 by the Count d'Artois, Marie Antoinette's brother-in-law; it's now used for temporary art exhibits. There's a bird sanctuary near the Grande Cascade (an artificial waterfall), but this area's main draw is its fabulous flowers, especially the irises in May and the roses in June. While parents relax and take in the blooms, kids can run off steam or have a close encounter with the resident birds—shy ducks and proud peacocks who roam around spreading their tails and screeching.

The Pré Catalan garden, in the center of the Bois, has kids' play areas and includes the Jardin de Shakespeare, with plants mentioned in the Bard's plays. In summer, open-air Shakespeare productions (some in English) are held near here. The grassy open areas of the Bois attract Paris-based U.S. expats who come to play baseball and football, and French people who play soccer and rugby. And there's plenty of room for just running around.

EATS FOR KIDS Within the park are two kid-friendly restaurants. You can take a little boat to **Le Châlet des Îles** (tel. 01–42–88–04–69), a magical—and expensive—restaurant on the island in the Lac Inférieur. There's parking nearby or you can walk from the La Muette métro stop. The delightful **Les Jardins de Bagatelle** restaurant in the Bagatelle gardens is a great spot with beautiful garden views (tel. 01–40–67–98–29). For a picnic in the Bois, there are food shops around the Sablons and Pont de Neuilly métro stops. For food see also Jardin d'Acclimatation (#45).

BOIS DE VINCENNES AND THE PARC FLORAL

Just east of Paris's city limits, the 500-plus-acre Bois de Vincennes (Vincennes Woods)—the ancient royal hunting grounds—is well worth a métro ride for its many family-friendly venues, particularly the Parc Floral de Paris and the 14th-century Château de Vincennes, the finest example of a medieval château in France.

Around the park's three lakes you can watch a puppet show, take a turn on a merry-go-round, eat *barbe à papa* (cotton candy), rent a paddleboat or a bicycle, or just sit on a bench and watch the world go by. Bike lanes, jogging paths, and sidewalks crisscross the park. You'll find plenty of places to picnic, as well as huge expanses of woods, grass, a bird sanctuary, a baseball field, a number of soccer fields, a horse-racing track (the Hippodrome de Vincennes), and even a working farm: the Ferme de Paris (rte. de Pésage, tel. 01–71–28–50–56) where kids can sometimes feed the animals.

The Bois's star attraction for families, though, is the Parc Floral de Paris. It has a grove of oak trees (meant to remind you of those 13th-century days when good King Louis dispensed justice under a huge oak tree near here), acres of lovely gardens, seasonal flower displays,

MAKE THE MOST OF YOUR TIME
The Parc Floral is an easy half-mile walk from the Château-de-Vincennes métro stop through the castle grounds. Enter the castle gates in front, walk over a splendid moat, and explore the beautifully renovated Sainte-Chapelle church, the castle keep, and some splendid 17th-century edifices. They're well worth seeing even if you don't take the castle tour. Through the back gates and across the street lies the Parc Floral. There are plenty of play options for youngsters throughout the bois, including sandboxes and small slides. Shady, uncrowded paths make this a great place to bring a child in a stroller.

Main entrance: av. Daumesnil, 12e. Métro: Porte Dorée, Château de Vincennes, Porte de Charenton

01–54–95–20–20 Parc Floral de Paris; www. parcfloraldeparis.com; www.boisdevincennes.com; www.chateau-vincennes.fr

Bois de Vincennes free, Parc Floral €5 ages 27 and up, €2.50 ages 7–26, extra charge for some attractions.

Bois daily 24 hrs; Parc Floral daily Apr–Sept 9:30–8, Oct–Jan 9:30–5, Feb 9:30–6, Mar 9:30–7

All ages

an amphitheater where you can catch a range of classical or jazz concerts on weekend afternoons through the summer and fall, several atriums with exotic plants, and the Maison de Paris Nature (House of Paris Nature), where you can learn about native Parisian flora and fauna and even visit a butterfly garden. There is also a train that traverses the gardens, and you can rent a four-person pedal cart for a family ride around the park.

The Parc Floral also contains one of the city's largest and best-kept play areas. Kids can climb on towers, ropes, and other structures; slide down long slides; and (for an extra fee) even play miniature golf on a course that features all the monuments of Paris in miniature. There's also a miniature pedal car race track and a Guignol puppet theater. The Théâtre Astral (tel. 01–43–71–31–10) offers high-quality kids' theater (extra charge). Free shows for kids, called *Les Pestacles*, are given from June to September (in French). Best of all, this park is quiet, clean, and rarely crowded.

KEEP IN MIND This is a huge park and to really benefit from all its forest and green space, you'll need to rent bikes. One reliable source is Location Vélo, a stand next to the Lac des Minimes that rents all types of bikes on weekends April–October, some with training wheels or baby seats and all in good condition. Another bike-rental operation is Paris Cycles near the Lac Daumesnil. All rent bikes for around €5 per hour, with discounts for longer rentals. There is also a Vélib' stand between the Château and the Parc Floral.

EATS FOR KIDS
Picnic in the Bois, which also has several snack bars, or try the restaurants in the Parc Floral: **Les Magnolias** (tel. 01–43–74–78–22) has good fixed-price lunches, afternoon tea, and a shady terrace; **Le Bosquet** (tel. 01–43–28–87–15) is a classy-looking but budget-priced cafeteria where sandwiches and fruit smoothies can be eaten on the premises or taken out for a picnic.

CATACOMBES

You don't have to have ghoulish tendencies to appreciate a visit to Paris's underground graveyard—but it helps. Walk down 90 steps to a huge complex of subterranean caverns stacked floor to ceiling with skeletons—around 6 million of them. Most have been artfully arranged, with row upon row of skulls set upon crossed tibias. The overall effect is like being on the set of a horror movie, an idea that's reinforced by the title "The Empire of the Dead" on the catacombs' brochures. Guides try to play down the macabre aspects, but with all those skeletons, what can they do?

Originally quarries, the catacombs yielded rocks used in the great buildings, roads, and aqueducts of the pre-Paris, Gallo-Roman stronghold of Lutetia. The quarries had been largely forgotten when, in 1785, someone had the idea to solve the problem of Paris's overcrowded cemeteries by placing skeletons in the underground caves. Several million skeletons from the Cimetière des Innocents (Cemetery of the Innocents) and others were then hauled here.

KEEP IN MIND You should judge whether your kids are likely to be intrigued or scared by all the bones. Guides light your way as you tour the shadowy caverns, but it's a good idea to bring your own pocket flashlight, as well as a jacket because it can get chilly.

MAKE THE MOST OF YOUR TIME After your close encounters with 6 million skeletons, you'll probably be ready for something a bit more cheerful. Les Cousins d'Alice (36 rue Daguerre, tel. 01–43–20–24–86) is a shop offering toys, books, party favors, CDs and cassettes. (Recordings of French songs are a good way to help your kids learn some French painlessly.) La Maison des Bonbons (14 rue Mouton-Duvernet, tel. 01–45–41–25–55) is just what the name says, the home of candy. You could also combine your visit to the Catacombes with a trip to the Observatoire de Paris to check out some Médaillons d'Arago (see #35).

 1 pl. Denfert-Rochereau, 14e.
Métro: Denfert-Rochereau

01–43–22–47–63

 €8 adults 27 and up,
€4 ages 14–26

 T–Su 10–5

 10 and up

A guide leads you through chilly, cramped corridors—each marked with the name of the street above it—and past stacks of bones. It's as though you're seeing Paris from a ghost's point of view. The indirect lighting casts shadows of bones onto the sides of the tunnels, reinforcing the Halloween atmosphere. Perhaps the most impressive aspect of the catacombs is their size, especially when you realize that you are taken through only a small part of the vast subterranean world, which has 65 kilometers (40 miles) of tunnels.

A small catacombs museum comes as a relief after your walk through the world of bones. Displays on the long history of this strange Paris underworld include its use as a secret headquarters of the Résistance (French resistance fighters) during Paris's occupation by German troops during World War II. Around 50,000 visitors tour the catacombs every year, proving that there are no dangers here, just the thrill of glimpsing Paris's creepy side—so different from the lively boulevards just a few feet above.

EATS FOR KIDS There are several restaurants along the nearby rue Daguerre, and a lively food market is held there on Sunday mornings. **Le Zeyer** (234 av. du Maine, on pl. d'Alésia, tel. 01–45–40–43–88), a big, bustling brasserie, prepares a delicious sole meunière (sole in butter sauce), classic *steak-frites* (steak with french fries), and tarte Tatin (upside-down apple tart). For food see also Médaillons d'Arago (#35).

CATHÉDRALE DE NOTRE-DAME-DE-PARIS

Small children may be disappointed not to see the Disney version of Quasimodo, the Hunchback of Notre-Dame, scrambling around on the cathedral's rooftops, but at least they can check out the gargoyles. France's most famous cathedral was built from 1163 to around 1345 on a spot that had already been considered holy for centuries. Take time to walk all the way around the cathedral to view the spectacular rose window above the main entrance; the gargoyles; the flying buttresses—added in the 14th century to support the structure's walls so that larger windows could be installed—and the magnificent Cloister Portal on the cathedral's north side, created in around 1250. A little park behind the cathedral has swings and benches and is always crowded with mothers, toddlers, and tourists.

Although most of Notre-Dame's original stained-glass windows have been lost over time and the church's interior can get crowded with tour groups, it's still a thrill to stand within the vast space where for centuries the kings and queens of France were crowned. The main appeal of Notre-Dame for most kids, however, is the chance to climb up to the cathedral's roof. The stairs—which are steep—begin at the base of the north tower. The reward for your climb

MAKE THE MOST OF YOUR TIME Just across the river on the Left Bank is Shakespeare and Company (37 rue de la Bûcherie, tel. 01–43–25–40–93, www.shakespeareco.org), a historic bookstore founded by George Whitman in 1951 and named in honor of a bookstore with the same name once run in another location by Sylvia Beach, a patron of Hemingway and other writers. The second Shakespeare and Co. is also a hangout for writers, many of whom give readings throughout the year. The shop overflows with new and used books in English.

Pl. du Parvis-de-Notre-Dame, 4e. Métro: Cité

 01-42-34-56-10; www. notredamedeparis.fr or www.notre-dame-de-paris.monuments-nationaux.fr

Cathedral free; tower €8 adults 26 and up, €5 ages 18–25

Cathedral daily 8–6:45; tower Apr–May and Sept, daily 10–6:30; June–Aug, M–F 10–6:30, Sa–Su 10–11 PM; Oct–Mar, daily 10–5:30; last access 45 mins before closing

 5 and up

(255 steps to the first level, then 125 more to the top of the south tower) is a spectacular view of the Seine and the Île de la Cité. Above you, in the south tower, the cathedral's great bell weighs 13 tons and is tolled only on momentous occasions.

In front of the church, the square known as the Parvis (from "Paradise") is the place to which all signposts throughout the country refer when they give distances to Paris. Beneath the Parvis, the aptly named Crypte Archéologique has vestiges of Gallo-Roman rooms. Thursday and Saturday nights from 9 to 10 there is a free show of projections on a giant transparent screen, with music, meant for kids and adults. There are also classical concerts held on certain weekdays at 8:30 PM; tickets are €18 for adults, free for kids 15 and under; check the schedule and reserve or purchase online.

KEEP IN MIND

Paris's poignant monument to the 200,000 people deported by the Nazis during World War II stands in the square de l'Île de France, at the tip of the Île de la Cité, behind Notre-Dame. The intentionally claustrophobic but open-air space has 200,000 little lights in memory of the deportees.

EATS FOR KIDS **Hippopotamus** (9 rue Lagrange, tel. 01–43–54–13–99) offers crayons, balloons, and a good fixed-price kids' menu. **La Fourmi Ailée** (8 rue du Fouarre, tel. 01–43–29–40–99), a tearoom/restaurant/library, has salads, vegetarian lasagna, and good pastries. **Gourmands de Notre Dame** (1 rue des Grands-Degrés, tel. 01–43–29–15–10) is the place to go for luscious ice cream in unusual flavors (pina colada, calvados apple tart). Stroll over to the Île Saint-Louis to sample the justifiably famous ice cream at **Berthillon** (31 rue St-Louis-en-Île, tel. 01–43–54–31–61, see (#44) for more about Berthillon).

CENTRE NATIONAL D'ART ET DE CULTURE GEORGES POMPIDOU

59

The Centre Pompidou (referred to by Parisians as "Beaubourg," after its neighborhood) was a big city–planning gamble. Former president Georges Pompidou and crew picked a vacant lot in the middle of Paris as the site for a "supermarket for culture" and created an edifice (designed by Renzo Piano and Richard Rogers) that looks like a kid might have built it using Legos and Tinkertoys. Today the center is popular among all sorts of Parisians, including children, who come for all sorts of reasons.

Thanks to its wacky architecture, the center is a hit with kids as soon as they see it. From the exterior, you see brightly painted ducts and supports, clearly showing why Parisians nicknamed this place Notre-Dame des Tuyeaux (Our Lady of the Pipes). Kids also appreciate the big square in front, which is always filled with fire-eaters, sword-swallowers, mimes, and musicians. It's an ongoing, free outdoor circus.

KEEP IN MIND

Check out the crazy fountain in the Square Igor-Stravinsky outside the Centre Pompidou. Designed by Niki de Saint-Phalle (the big red lips that squirt at you) and Jean Tinguely (the mysterious robotic metal contraptions), it shows even the youngest kids how much fun contemporary art can be.

EATS FOR KIDS

The center's top-floor **Restaurant Georges,** reached by escalator or the glass-walled elevator, has great views and a large outdoor terrace, while the in-house **Café Mezzanine** and **Kiosk** caféteria offer lots of low-priced choices. **Dame Tartine** (2 rue Brisemiche, tel. 01–42–77–32–22) serves quiches, salads, and other affordable treats, and its terrace overlooks the wacky fountain in square Igor-Stravinsky. For food see also Jardin des Halles (#43), Musée de la Poupée (#31), Musée d'Art et d'Histoire du Judaïsme (#33), and Place des Vosges and the Marais (#6).

Rue Beaubourg, 4e.
Métro: Hotel-de-Ville, Rambuteau

01-44-78-12-33; www.
centrepompidou.fr and www.junior.
centrepompidou.fr (Web site for kids)

Center free; art museum €12
adults 18 and up; kids' films €6;
kids' classes €10; special exhibitions €14 adults 18 and up

Center W–M 11–10, art museum
W–M 11–9, kids' gallery W–M 11–7

2 and up, kids'
gallery 2–12

Visitors flock inside to do research in the public library, see films in the movie theaters or live performances in the Grande Salle (Large Hall), view the stunning collection in the Musée National d'Art Moderne (National Museum of Modern Art), or just appreciate the breathtaking views of central Paris. Even small children respond to the art here, especially the Alexander Calder mobiles, the weird mechanical structures of Jean Tinguely, and the vibrantly colored paintings of Matisse, Léger, and Soutine. The museum has so many works of art that it rotates them all the time, so you never know what will be on display here.

In La Galerie des Enfants, a gallery space geared to kids, you'll find special interactive exhibits, all exploring different examples of contemporary art, as well as a wide choice of creative workshops for kids 2–5 or 6–10. Every Wednesday at 2:30, the center's Cinema 2 shows films for kids 5–12 (in French, reservations possible, tel. 01–44–78–44–22). And if it's kid-pleasing vistas you're after, take an elevator that runs through a glass tube up the west side of the building. The view is spectacular, especially at sunset.

MAKE THE MOST OF YOUR TIME For kids, guided
tours and all sorts of creative arts workshops are held in the Galerie des Enfants on Wednesdays, weekends, and school holidays, except in August. Special activities for families (shows, guided tours, and workshops, in French) are offered on Sundays (€10 for one adult and one child). For information and reservations in English, check www.centrepompidou.fr, English version, and search "Family Sundays" or "children," or call 01–44–78–49–13.

If there's one Paris street that people have heard of, it's the avenue des Champs-Élysées—"Les Champs" to Parisians. This wide street, first built in 1667 as an approach to the royal palace in the Tuileries, was widened, beautified, and given its current name (which means "Elysian Fields") in the 19th century, when it became known as the most beautiful avenue in the world.

In the 20th century, however, the avenue evolved into a bustling, high-rent commercial district whose sidewalks literally became parking lots. Beginning in the 1990s, a decade-long renovation project reclaimed sidewalks for pedestrians and lined the avenue with tall trees, and the Champs became pleasant to stroll down again. In many ways, though, it's been a victim of its success. Rents are now so high that only major retailers can afford them. The world's biggest Adidas store (22 av. Champs-Élysées) opened here in 2006, while many of the movie theaters and smaller shops that once lined the avenue have closed. In 2007, the city launched a campaign to try to preserve the avenue from becoming a glorified shopping mall by limiting any more mega-stores from opening along it.

MAKE THE MOST OF YOUR TIME

A few minutes' walk away is the Musée Jacquemart-André (158 bd. Haussmann, tel. 01–45–62–11–59, www.musee-jacquemart-andre.com), which houses the private art collection of a 19th-century couple who favored Old Masters, including Rembrandt and Botticelli. Paintings are displayed in a magnificent yet intimate private mansion that demonstrates the elegance of the Champs-Élysées neighborhood in the mid-1800s. Rent an audio guide to get the most out of your visit. The lovely in-house café (open even to those not visiting the museum) is a favorite choice for lunch, brunch, and especially their famous afternoon tea.

Pl. de la Concorde to Arc de Triomphe, 8e.
Métro: Franklin-D.-Roosevelt, George-V,
Champs-Élysées–Clemenceau

 Free

 Daily 24 hrs

 08–92–68–30–30 Office de Tourisme;
www.parisinfo.com

All ages

A stroll down this famous street is still a thrill, if only for the views of the Arc de Triomphe at the top of the hill with the broad avenue stretching down to the place de la Concorde. The shady sidewalks are wide enough to walk comfortably along (not often the case in Paris), and Paris's oldest Guignol puppet theater (opened in 1818) still draws kids at the Rond Point des Champs-Élysées, a peaceful retreat in this busy neighborhood. A famous stamp market is held in the park three times weekly.

And of course there's the shopping. If you have a yen for a US$2,000 handbag or a new Mercedes, you can find them on the Champs, or you could visit Virgin Megastore (52 av. Champs-Élysées) and the similar FNAC (74 av. Champs-Élysées) for CDs, books, and all kinds of electronic goods that appeal to teens, as well as the Disney Store (44 av. Champs-Élysées) for the Disney-character-loving younger set. Paris's Elysian Fields is still a paradise for shoppers.

EATS FOR KIDS

Restaurants right on the avenue include **Planet Hollywood** (78 av. Champs-Élysées, tel. 01–53–83–78–27) for burgers and other U.S.-style treats, **Pizza Pino** (33 av. Champs-Élysées, tel. 01–40–74–01–12) for tasty pizza, and the **Ladurée** pastry shop (75 av. Champs-Élysées, tel. 01–40–75–08–75), a Paris institution and elegant tearoom. For food see also École Lenôtre (#51).

KEEP IN MIND Note that the Champs slopes steeply up to the Arc de Triomphe, so if you have small children, start your stroll on the Arc end of the avenue to avoid the uphill. Guignol puppet shows (€3.50, www.theatreguignol.fr), are performed Wednesday, Saturday, Sunday, and holidays at 3, 4, and 5 PM, and the stamp and pin market is held on Thursday, Saturday, and Sunday. Nearby, you can take a peek through heavily guarded gates at the Palais d'Élysée (France's White House) and at the U.S. Embassy.

CHÂTEAU DE VERSAILLES

57

To kids, the Château de Versailles and its over-the-top gilded luxury may seem more like a theme park than the palace of French kings. While most children aren't overly impressed by its rich furnishings and sumptuously decorated rooms, they do find much to interest them, both in the château and especially outside it.

Even kids can't resist the dazzling Galerie des Glaces (Hall of Mirrors); the Salon d'Apollo (Sun King's Throne Room), dripping with gold; and the Chambre du Roi (King's Bedroom), big enough for an army. Watch for images of the sun, in honor of Louis XIV (the Sun King). Louis was jealous of another château, Vaux-le-Vicomte, which belonged to his own finance minister, so he had Versailles built, using the same architect (Le Vau), to prove who was boss.

Outside the château, a vast formal garden—created by the architect Le Nôtre (designer of Vaux-le-Vicomte's gardens and Paris's Tuileries)—is filled with statues, fountains, and elegant perspectives. The garden and surrounding park are great places for kids to run around. You can tour the park by bicycle (rentals at the Porte St-Antoine entrance and near

KEEP IN MIND Versailles is 20 kilometers (12 miles) southwest of Paris. Take the RER commuter train, line C, to the Versailles–Rive Gauche stop; around 60 trains a day run Monday–Saturday, and 35 on Sunday. By car (30 minutes), take the A13 highway west to the Versailles–Château exit.

MAKE THE MOST OF YOUR TIME Free individual audio guides are available in English for kids 8 and older at the château's main entrance ; or make reservations for a guided tour in English. Excellent tours for kids and families as well as kids' workshops are given in French (tel. 01–30–83–77–47). Don't miss Les Grandes Eaux Musicales, when the park's fountains are turned on and set to music (dates, hours, and costs vary), and the Grande Fête de la Nuit sound-and-light extravaganzas held in summer. The money-saving Passport Versailles (for ages 18 and over) can be purchased in advance at train stations, some museums, and other locations.

Town of Versailles

01–30–83–78–00;
www.chateauversailles.fr

Château only €15 adults 18 and up; Domaine Marie-Antoinette €10 adults; extra charge for tours, special events, and classes; Passport Versailles (château and all attractions) €18 adults, on water music days and musical stroll days €25; first Sunday of every month Nov–Mar admission free for all tours; park free

Château Apr–Oct, T–Su 9–6:30; Nov–Mar, T–Su 9–5:30; park Apr–Oct, 8 AM–8:30 PM, Nov–Mar 8–6; hrs vary for other attractions

3 and up

the Grand Canal), electric car (ask at the entrance for details) or on a little mock train that starts from the château's north terrace—a great option for tired little—or big—feet. Paddling a four-person boat around the Grand Canal is also fun (March–October, rental stand at La Petite Venise). You can visit the château's splendid Grandes Écuries (Great Stables), too, now home to pampered horses as well as a school of equestrian arts that regularly presents shows to the public.

Louis XV built the Petit Trianon, an elegant little château in the park, for his mistress, Madame de Pompadour; the ill-fated King Louis XVI later gave it to Marie-Antoinette. Young kids like the Hameau de la Reine (Queen's Hamlet), a mock farm created by Marie-Antoinette so she could play at being a shepherdess (albeit one surrounded by servants to do the dirty work). Today, at the petting zoo here, kids 5–12 who'd like to play at being Marie-Antoinette can sign up for an afternoon (Wednesday–Saturday) of brushing a donkey and feeding chickens (€10 adults, kids free; reservations tel. 01–39–49–18–18, www.ferme-pedagogique.com).

EATS FOR KIDS La Flotille (tel. 01–39–51–41–58), next to the Grand Canal, has a restaurant section (lunch only) with a good fixed-price menu for parents and a tasty kids' menu, as well as a cheaper brasserie section (open all day) and sandwiches for a park-bench picnic. In summer you can eat on the outdoor terrace overlooking the canal. The park also has several snack stands. At **Sister's Café** (15 rue des Réservoirs, tel. 01–30–21–21–22), a relaxed, friendly restaurant, you can sample U.S. treats like chicken wings, quesadillas, and a hearty brunch in the domain of the Sun King.

CITÉ DE LA MUSIQUE

Ever had a yen to play in a gamelan (an Indonesian orchestra)? At the Cité de la Musique (Music Center) complex, the whole family can take a gamelan class or a workshop featuring world instruments, attend a concert featuring some of the world's best musicians, check out Beethoven's very own clavichord, and see about 4,500 rare musical instruments from around the globe. Also home to France's prestigious Conservatoire Nationale de Musique (National Music Conservatory), the Cité de la Musique is one of the jewels in the crown of Paris's ambitious La Villette development project. It's a must for music-lovers.

The center's Musée de la Musique (Music Museum) contains the conservatory's huge collection of musical instruments as well as scale models of opera houses and concert halls with all their backstage equipment. Everything in this museum is designed with kids in mind. As you enter the museum, you receive headphones equipped with an infrared device that senses when you're standing in front of an instrument and starts a tape with commentary and an extract of a virtuoso player's performance on that particular instrument. Headphones with commentary in English are available. Often kids don't want to take off the headphones when

MAKE THE MOST OF YOUR TIME The Ateliers Musical en Famille (family music workshop) classes are held in French on Sundays, October–June (€10 per adult, €7 per child). You can also take classes in other instruments. Kid-oriented concerts are usually given on Wednesdays at 3 and Saturdays at 11 (€7). On Wednesdays, Saturdays, Sundays, and school holidays, look for classes and special guided tours of the museum for kids. Top musicians perform regularly at concerts in the 1,000-seat concert hall.

221 av. Jean-Jaurès, 19e.
Métro: Porte-de-Pantin

01–44–84–44–84;
www.cite-musique.fr

Museum €6.50 ages 18 and over; extra charge for concerts, temporary exhibits, and classes

T–Sa 12–6, Su 10–6

6 and up

their visit ends. Special guided visits (in French) bring the world of music to life through games and stories, and classes for kids, or kids and their families, are offered regularly. Children ages 6 and up, for example, can learn how to play a range of traditional world instruments and really impress their friends back home. Spectacles Jeune Public (theater-music-dance performances for young audiences) are organized almost every week. After the show, kids usually get to sit and chat with the performers.

As for those hands-on music classes, they're for families with children 6 or over who'd like to learn to play one of the 20 or so gamelan instruments, the *sanza* (African thumb piano), or the South American *siku* flute. Never played an instrument before? Don't worry; sit on the floor and let the friendly teachers (most of whom speak English) explain the gongs, xylophones, drums, flute, and other world instruments. After a while, you'll hear yourself and your family making music together. Music is the universal language, after all, and the center is a great place to learn how to speak it.

KEEP IN MIND Visiting this and all the other kid-friendly attractions in and around the Parc de la Villette (#11), including the Cité des Enfants (#55) and Cité des Sciences et de l'Industrie (#54) could easily fill up a day, but if you're pressed for time you could also combine a trip here with a cruise on the Canal St-Martin (see Paris Canal, #8). If you do this, go first to the Cité des Enfants, then visit the Cité des Sciences, and then you'll just have time for a quick visit to the Cité de la Musique before the canal cruise starts nearby at 2:30 PM.

EATS FOR KIDS
Café de la Musique adjoining the Cité (213 av. Jean-Jaurès, tel. 01–48–03–15–91) is a trendy but casual brasserie with an outdoor terrace, serving classic French cuisine, homemade fries, and a good Sunday brunch. For food see also Cité des Sciences et de l'Industrie (#54), Cité des Enfants (#55), and Parc de la Villette (#11).

CITÉ DES ENFANTS

This children's museum within Paris's futuristic Cité des Sciences et de l'Industrie complex (see #54) is without a doubt one of Paris's top stops for kids. Divided into three sections—one for ages 2–7, one for ages 5–12, and one for special exhibitions (generally for kids 5–12)—the Cité des Enfants takes very seriously the idea that kids should have fun while they learn. The innovative special exhibitions, including a recent one on light and shadows, are both thought-provoking and entertaining for kids.

In the age-specific sections of the Cité, hands-on exhibits (each section gives children more than 150 different things to do) are so colorful and exciting that kids tend to run around the whole time, poking and pushing and pulling. Although children must be accompanied by an adult, no more than two adults per family are allowed in at one time, so if you're an adult, you are definitely going to be in the minority here.

EATS FOR KIDS In addition to the food outlets within and just outside the museum complex, there are shops on the avenue Corentin-Cariou where you can buy picnic goodies to eat in the Parc de la Villette (#11); for food also see the Cité de la Musique (#56) and Cité des Sciences et de l'Industrie (#54).

MAKE THE MOST OF YOUR TIME The children's museum is open for four or five (depending on the time of year) 90-minute visits each day, usually beginning at 9:45. Only a limited number of people are allowed inside at each session, so it's a good idea to come here first when you arrive at the Cité des Sciences et de l'Industrie and get tickets for the next available session—or you can call or visit the Web site the day before to make a reservation. Try to avoid Saturday and Wednesday afternoons, when many day-care centers and schools bring groups here and the staff seems to let in more kids than usual.

Cité des Sciences et de l'Industrie, 30 av. Corentin-Cariou, 19e. Métro: Corentin-Cariou

 01–40–05–80–00 for information; 08–92–69–70–72 for reservations (in French); www.cite-sciences.fr

 €6 price includes 3-D film at Cinema Louis Lumièe; €15.50 for package including la Géode (see #54)

 T–Sa 9:30–6, Su 9:45–7

 2 and up

Exhibits for younger kids are simple to use as well as instructive, tactile, and fun. Kids might try their hand at a huge hand-operated grain grinder that illustrates how wheat becomes flour, step on a dance floor to activate a video camera that lets them see themselves hop around, or put on hard hats at a construction site and build huge structures with foam bricks. A favorite is a whole section that lets kids get as wet as they like while diverting flowing water through channels (plastic lab coats provided).

Older kids might test their own senses of smell, sight, touch, and hearing; get a hands-on lesson in how satellites work; try out the equipment in a mini–sound studio; watch butterflies emerge from their cocoons; create their own TV show; or study their own balance and breathing—and that's just the beginning. How much more fun can learning get?

KEEP IN MIND One trick to help kids avoid crowding at the most popular exhibits in the age-specific sections is to start your visit with the exhibits farthest from the main entrance and then work your way back. Exhibits for two-year-olds were added to the section for younger kids in 2007 and many new additions to the section for older kids were added in 2008. This constantly evolving museum has been so successful that it has been expanded to five times its original size.

CITÉ DES SCIENCES ET DE L'INDUSTRIE

54

When you first spot the high-tech exterior of this huge museum complex it's hard to believe that the site was once home to a ramshackle slaughterhouse in one of Paris's grubbiest neighborhoods. The Cité des Sciences et de l'Industrie (Museum of Science and Industry), a product of inspired city planning, shows that Paris has its foot firmly planted in the 21st century. Everything about this place is cutting-edge, from its architecture to its user-friendly exhibits.

The museum's huge, 9,500-square-meter (102,000-square-foot) Explora section, which was completely updated in 2007, has almost 20 departments full of interactive gadgets that most of us never got to play with in science class. They're all designed to teach schoolchildren (and adults) fun things about all sorts of subjects, including images, outer space, sounds, math, innovation, the plant world, cars, energy, and lots more. Two favorites for kids are the display on sound deflectors, which lets you whisper and be heard 15 meters (50 feet) away; and the exhibit that lets you make Mona Lisa speak in your own voice. There's even

MAKE THE MOST OF YOUR TIME If you'd like your children to interact with French kids, take them to the Cafézoïde near the Cité des Sciences (92 bis, Quai-de-la-Loire, tel. 01–42–38–26–37, www.cafezoide.asso.fr). Created by a former teacher, Cafézoïde is Paris's only café just for kids. Lots of different activities are organized daily (painting, playing musical instruments, dance classes) and you can have lunch or sample pastries and homemade waffles in the afternoon. Kids under 8 must be accompanied by a parent.

Parc de la Villette, 30 av. Corentin-Cariou, 19e. Métro: Porte de la Villette

€10 adults 26 and up, €8 ages 7–25; €21 adults 26 and up, €19 ages 7–25, including special exhibits, Géode, Planétarium, Biodiversité, and other special attractions

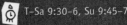

T–Sa 9:30–6, Su 9:45–7

01-40-05-80-00 (English message available); www.cite-sciences.fr

3 and up

a whole museum, the Cité des Enfants (#55), just for 2- to 12-year-olds, and the Cité des Sciences regularly organizes creative, kid-friendly temporary exhibits.

You could spend days just exploring Explora, but the museum complex offers much more. The gleaming silver Géode dome shows mind-boggling IMAX films on a 1,000-square-meter (more than 10,000-square-foot) hemispherical screen, and the 300-seat Le Planétarium presents shows on the galaxy. You can tour the Argonaute, a spy submarine built during the Cold War for the French navy, and check out a space-age greenhouse. The Louis Lumière cinema shows 3-D films (in French and English), and the Cineaxe—which seats 56 and is billed as the biggest simulator in the world—takes you and your kids on virtual trips, perhaps into outer space or to the bottom of the sea, in a screening room that moves along with the 3-D images you're watching. Cool! This is one museum where your children are almost certain to play happily for hours without whining once—and they're sure to learn something, too.

EATS FOR KIDS
The museum complex contains several places to eat, including **Aux Pains Perdus**, a self-service cafeteria where everyone in your group can taste individual portions of classic French fare, and **Le Hublot,** which offers salads, daily specials, and yummy chocolate mousse cake; both restaurants are on level 2 of the Cité. A branch of **Hippopotamus** (28 av. Corentin-Cariou, tel. 01–44–72–15–15) has grilled chicken or beef brochettes, fries, and other kid pleasers; and **Cafézöide** (see Make the Most of Your Time) offers more than just a meal. For food see also Cité des Enfants (#55) and Parc de la Villette (#11).

KEEP IN MIND
Long lines can build up at the planetarium, the Cineaxe, and the Géode before each day's shows begin. All shows are in French, but the Géode has free headphones with commentary in English. In any case, the images are so stunning that kids should enjoy themselves even if they can't understand French.

DISNEYLAND PARIS AND WALT DISNEY STUDIOS PARK

The Magic Kingdom is an easy trip from Paris, and the resort now includes two theme parks: the original Disneyland Paris and Walt Disney Studios Park, which focuses on filmmaking. You're sure to find something to please everyone in the family.

Disneyland Paris is a reduced version of Disneyland in the United States, but there's still plenty for kids to enjoy. Best choices for the younger crowd include Alice's Maze (where kids love seeing their parents get stuck in tiny openings), and the Mad Hatter's Teacups and Peter Pan's Flight rides, as well as the afternoon parade of huge floats featuring Disney's most famous characters (check posted times and come early to get a good spot). Older kids will no doubt favor the big-thrill rides, especially Space Mountain and Indiana Jones and the Temple of Peril, both of which have age and height restrictions. Make sure to pick up the brochure at the ticket booth that lists the rides along with symbols that designate specific requirements.

MAKE THE MOST OF YOUR TIME

The quickest (40 minutes) way to cover the 32 kilometers (20 miles) east from Paris to Disneyland is by RER commuter train, line A. Combination Disneyland–transport tickets are sold in Paris métro and train stations. By car, take the A4 highway toward Marne-la-Vallée; exit at Parc Disneyland.

EATS FOR KIDS Both parks are filled with snack bars and restaurants in a variety of styles and price ranges. If possible, avoid having lunch during the peak period of 12–1:30, or make reservations in advance. Disney Village, a commercial development just outside the parks' gates (hold on to your entrance tickets to get back into the parks), has several restaurants (Annette's Diner, The Steakhouse, and other American-style eateries); all are usually less crowded than those inside the parks.

Marne-la-Vallée

 For each theme park €53 ages 12 and up, €45 children 3–11; ticket for both parks €67 ages 12 and up, €57 children 3–11; two-day and three-day passes also available. Check online for specials.

01–60–30–60–30; www.disneylandparis.com

In general, Disneyland Apr–June and Sept–Oct, daily 10–8; July–Aug, daily 10 AM–11 PM; Nov–Mar, M–F 10–7, Sa–Su 10–8; Walt Disney Studios closes earlier

 3 and up

In Walt Disney Studios Park, the Catastrophe Canyon ride whizzes you through a film shoot, Cars takes you on the fast track, and Crush's Coaster jerks and spins you through Nemo's world. You can also see some spectacular special effects and amazing stunts. The main drawbacks of either park are that younger kids are bombarded with so many stimuli that they may at some point burst into tears through sheer overload, while older kids get frustrated if they have to wait in line for an hour to enjoy a ride that's over in less than four minutes. Everyone seems to forget these problems, though, when they see the fabulous fireworks display over Sleeping Beauty's castle, with Tinkerbell flitting around overhead leaving a trail of pixie dust.

KEEP IN MIND To avoid long lines at the park entrance, buy your tickets in advance (online, by telephone, or in various Paris locations). Special offers are often available. Free Fast Passes allow you to use a special "fast" line for top rides. Go to a ride, put your park entrance ticket into the Fast Pass machine there, and you'll receive a Fast Pass marked with a specific time. Come back to the ride at that time and take the Fast Pass line to get on the ride. Go to the top rides soon after you enter the park to get your Fast Pass.

DOUBLE FOND

You sit down, your waiter brings you a multicolored drink, and—presto!—your glass disappears right before your very eyes! What kind of place *is* this?

The Double Fond is a café-theater for people who love magic tricks. (The French name refers to the double, or false, bottom on a trick box.) What sets the shows here apart from big-time magic extravaganzas in huge auditoriums is that the tricks are performed in a fairly small space right in front of you, and everyone in the audience gets a chance to participate. Kids are encouraged to get in on the act, especially at the matinees, designed especially for them. The emphasis is on card tricks and other classic sleight-of-hand numbers that have eternal appeal for youngsters. You and your children can enjoy a part of the city's rich and varied theater scene even if you don't speak French, since the shows are based mainly on gestures rather than language. To get the full benefit of a performance if you don't speak French, ask whether a special show in English can be arranged for a group (call in advance for information). You may be able to join a group that is already scheduled.

KEEP IN MIND If your family loves magic shows, you should also check out Metamorphosis (3 quai de Montebello, tel. 01–43–54–08–08, www.metamorphosis-spectacle.fr, reservations necessary), a theater-restaurant in a houseboat on the Seine, created by a professional magician who stages high-quality magic shows T–Sa 9:30 PM (€30 and €16 for children under 13) and special shows geared to kids on Sunday afternoons at 3 (€16). You can have a meal on the boat before the show (€38 or €32 under 13, for the meal and show), and snacks are available after the matinee (€6). The copious Sunday brunch (served at 12:30) includes quesadillas, smoked salmon, scrambled eggs, and pastries (€38 or €32 under 13).

1 pl. du Marché-Ste-Catherine, 4e.
Métro: St-Paul

 €10 matinees, €20 evenings; some shows extra

 Shows Th–F 9 PM, Sa 9 PM and 11 PM; matinees W 4:30, Su 4:30 except mid-July–Aug, Sa 2:30 and 4:30; special shows sometimes at other times

 01–42–71–40–20; www.doublefond.com

 Matinees 5–12, evenings 10 and up

You can sit at the tall stools in the downstairs bar with your eyes glued to the magician's hands just inches in front of your face and you still won't be able to tell how the magician manages to make that ace of spades turn up where you least expect it. That is, you probably won't be able to figure it out unless you've taken one of the magic classes offered here. You can opt for a scheduled group class, a private one-hour session in which you learn at least two cool tricks, or a private group class just for your family. These classes are in French, but when you make your reservations (essential), ask whether a class in English is available. Most instructors speak English. Everyone in the family can learn how to trick your friends back home. Invite a few people over, serve them something to drink, and—you got it!—no more glass. Tell them you learned it in Paris.

For more magic tricks, visit the nearby Musée de la Magie et Musée des Automates (see #32).

EATS FOR KIDS

Double Fond serves drinks but no meals, except at special dinner-theater shows. **Columbus Café** (25 rue Vieille-de-Temple, tel. 01–42–72–20–11) is a good choice for yummy American-style cookies and muffins before or after the show. For food see also Place des Vosges (#6) and Musée de la Magie et Musée des Automates (#32).

MAKE THE MOST OF YOUR TIME

Double Fond's magic classes include a special 45-minute class for kids given just after each matinee performance (€10), a private one-hour class adapted to the individual student in which you are guaranteed to learn at least two new tricks (€62); a one-hour group class or series of classes (in French) for anyone 12 and over, held on Thursdays at 7 PM (€22 one session, €80 for four sessions); and private classes tailored to individuals or groups (prices vary); tel. 01–42–71–40–20 for details and reservations.

ÉCOLE LENÔTRE ATELIERS DES PETITS MAGICIENS GOURMETS

How would you like your kids to whip up a chocolate mousse for your next dinner party? They might learn how to do just that and a whole lot more at this cooking school for kids organized by Lenôtre, one of France's best-known names in gourmet cuisine and pastry.

The 90-minute classes are given on Wednesday afternoons (in French) in the palatial Pavillon Élysée-Lenôtre, a stone-and-glass structure built for the Paris world's fair in 1900. It's definitely a temple to gastronomy. The kitchens, as you might expect, have every possible cooking gadget on hand. Classes, each led by a highly trained Lenôtre chef, are limited to eight kids, so every child gets plenty of chances to ask questions and get to know fellow food-loving classmates. Classes for kids 8–11 or 12–17 are offered, and there is one two-hour pastry class for 8–11 year olds (accompanied by one parent, if Mom or Dad wants to join in). These very hands-on classes show kids how much fun cooking can be, while also teaching them basic techniques of classic French cuisine. Younger children won't be asked to use any dangerous kitchen equipment (specially designed recipes avoid the need for

KEEP IN MIND

Le Comptoir, also within the Pavillon Élysée-Lenôtre (tel. 01–42–65–85–10), is a shop for food lovers. You'll find all kinds of books on food; a wide choice of wine, teas, coffees, olive oils, vinegars, and more; and even some classy cooking utensils to use when you whip up your own gourmet feast.

EATS FOR KIDS The on-site **Café Lenôtre** (tel. 01–42–65–85–10 for reservations) offers creative cuisine based on the day's food-market offerings, as well as luscious desserts and an elegant outdoor terrace. At **Misia** (5 rue du Commandant-Rivière, tel. 01–42–56–38–74), the evening menu for kids features smaller portions of everything on the gourmet regular menu. While kids' menus in most French restaurants are limited to tried-and-true combos like *jambon-frites* (ham and fries), here adventurous kids might sample beef rolls with Asian spices or sautéed frogs' legs with wild mushrooms. For food see also Champs-Élysées (#58) and Palais de la Découverte (#14).

Pavillon Élysée Lenôtre,
10 av. des Champs-Élysées, 8e.
Métro: Champs-Élysées–Clemenceau

 €40 kids 8–11,
€80 kids 12–17

W 2–3:30 or 4–5:30

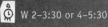 01-42-65-97-60; www.lenotre.fr

8–17

that), but will sometimes do some chopping under the chef's watchful eye. The most-used tools in the class for 8- to 11-year-olds are the whisk and the wooden spoon. Although most of the chefs speak at least some English, children need to speak at least some French to be able to follow what's going on.

Each class focuses on a particular dish. Younger kids might learn how to make apple crumble or *chouquettes* (sugar-coated cream-puff pastries), while older kids might learn how to wow you with their very own *beaux'hommes à la coque* (eggs prepared with comté cheese, ham, and baby vegetables), *croustillant de dorade aux légumes confites* (crispy *dorade* with slow-cooked vegetables), or *velouté au chocolat* (soft-centered chocolate cake). The best part is that kids get to eat their creations after the class and, if there's any left over (unlikely), bring some home (or to the hotel) to share.

MAKE THE MOST OF YOUR TIME For cuisine-loving moms and dads, Lenôtre gives classes for adults (in French) year-round. These classes (six or seven people) last 3½ hours or more and cost from around €135 (chocolate éclairs, for example) to €330 (for an all-day class in which you learn to prepare a gala dinner). You do get to eat what you prepare, not to mention wow your family and guests at your next party. For any class, contact the school or check the Web site well in advance to find out what dishes are being taught when and to reserve a place.

FONDATION CLAUDE MONET

You can spend a day in the country and enjoy the arts, too, in Giverny, a pretty little village on the bank of the Seine west of Paris that was home to the Impressionist painter Claude Monet from 1883 until his death in 1926. Tops on the list is a visit to Monet's house, now a museum (but called the Claude Monet Foundation), which an international group of Monet fans saved from decay after 1980. You'll get a feel for what life was like when the artist lived and worked here and made the house a gathering place for his artist friends. Coming here also lets kids who've seen Monet's water lily paintings in the Musée d'Orsay (see #27) or the Musée de l'Orangerie (#29) make the connection between those works and the real person who created them in the nearby garden.

The first thing you'll notice is Monet's love of color. The house, set in a luxuriant garden, has peachy-pink walls and deep green shutters on the outside. On the inside, rooms have been restored as much as possible to what they were when Monet lived in them. Even small children should like the buttercup-yellow dining room with its big farmhouse table, yellow

KEEP IN MIND Another Giverny attraction, the Musée des Impressionnismes Giverny (99 rue Claude-Monet, tel. 02–32–51–94–65, www.museedesimpressionnismesgiverny.com), holds a permanent collection and changing exhibits of works by Impressionist artists. A free booklet (in English) takes you on a fun tour. Guided tours in English of the museum and Giverny are available. The museum also organizes family visits and workshops in the museum garden for children between 4 and 12 years old accompanied by a parent. Kids get to learn about Impressionist techniques using finger paints to create their own colorful landscapes.

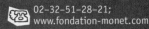 84 rue Claude-Monet, Giverny

02-32-51-28-21;
www.fondation-monet.com

€6 ages 12 and up, €3.50 ages
7–11; €12 ages 12 and up,
€8.50 ages 7–11 for tickets including admission to the Musée
des Impressionnismes Giverny

 Apr–Oct, daily 9:30–6

7 and up

chimneypiece, and Monet's favorite Japanese prints on the walls. Renoir, Sisley, Cézanne, Manet, and Pissarro all came here to share the excellent and copious meals Monet favored, and to debate about art. Kids should appreciate the cheery kitchen, too, with its gorgeous bright-blue Portuguese tiles and more gleaming copper saucepans than you ever thought existed. You can also visit the painter's studio, furnished like a den with armchairs and little tables. Although you'll see no original paintings here now, reproductions of Monet's works hang on the walls to remind you of the images that the artist created in this place.

Kids should enjoy a tour of the sprawling gardens, with its paths winding through banks of flowers, its water-lily-filled ponds, and its picturesque Japanese bridge immortalized in Monet's works. You'll feel like you've walked inside one of his paintings.

EATS FOR KIDS
Les Nymphéas (48 rue Claude-Monet, tel. 02–32–21–20–31) serves good fixed-price menus, salads, and ice cream. The welcoming **Musée des Impressionnismes Giverny's Terra Café** (see Keep in Mind) offers light meals and afternoon pastries; eat outside on the terrace and let the kids run in the garden.

MAKE THE MOST OF YOUR TIME Giverny is 87 kilometers (54 miles) west of Paris. By rail, take the Rouen-Le Havre train from Paris's Gare Saint-Lazare and get off at the Vernon stop, from which you can take a taxi or bus to Giverny, around 5 kilometers (3 miles) away. You can also rent bicycles at the station in Vernon and bike to Giverny. From the train station, cross the bridge over the Seine and turn right. By car, take the A13 autoroute (toll highway) from Paris toward Le Havre, and get off at the Vernon exit. From Vernon, take the D191 and the D5 roads to Giverny.

FONTAINEBLEAU

If you'd like to spend a day in the country, do as the Parisians do and head for Fontainebleau, a pleasant town with a historic château ringed by a vast forest. And it's only an hour from Notre-Dame.

Fontainebleau's château was built in the 12th century as a hunting lodge, but if you're thinking rustic retreat, think again: this has always been the domain of French royalty. King François I added huge Italian-style rooms and galleries in the 16th century, other kings added their own embellishments, the great 17th-century garden designer Le Nôtre created terraces and fountains here, and Napoléon chose Fontainebleau over Versailles. A visit to this lavishly furnished château with its elegant gardens is like a quick trip through French history.

The château's Cour des Adieux (Courtyard of Good-Byes, where Napoléon said his *adieux* to his troops in 1814) has one of the few *jeu de paume* (palm game) courts left in France. On Saturdays you can watch expert players demonstrate this ancestor of tennis

EATS FOR KIDS
Picnic in the forest or try **Au Délice Impérial** (1 rue Grande, tel. 01–64–22–20–70), a pastry shop/restaurant, **Pizza-Pazza** (1 rue des Bouchers, tel. 01–60–72–05–61) for tasty pizza and pasta, or **Le Franklin** (20 rue Grande, tel. 01–64–22–28–73), a cozy bistro. There's a **food market** near Saint-Louis church on Tuesday, Friday, and Sunday mornings.

KEEP IN MIND
To rent bicycles, canoes, and kayaks, contact Top Loisirs (16 rue Sylvain-Collinet, tel. 01–60–74–08–50, www.toploisirs.fr); reservations necessary. Top Loisirs also gives rock-climbing classes and organizes other sports-related activities. La Petite Reine (36 rue des Sablons, tel. 01–60–74–57–57) rents bikes. The tourist office (4 rue Royal, tel. 01–60–74–99–99, www.fontainebleau-tourisme.com) rents bikes and has free maps and other practical information, including information about local equestrian centers and sites for rock-climbing and bouldering. Reelbooks (9 rue Ferrare, tel. 01–64–22–85–85) has books in English.

42 miles southeast of Paris

 01-60-74-99-99, www.fontainebleau-tourisme.com (tourist office); 01-60-71-50-70, www.musee-chateau-fontainebleau.fr (château)

 Forest and château gardens free, château €10 ages 18 and over

 Château W–Su; Apr–Sept, 9:30–6; Oct–Mar, 9:30–5; gardens open daily 9–sunset

Château 4 and up; gardens all ages

and squash. The château and its gardens are well worth a visit (be sure to bring some bread to feed the goldfish in the canals), but for active families, Fontainebleau's main draw is its forest, which covers about 14,000 acres and is considered one of the most beautiful and diverse forests in France. UNESCO has classified it a "biosphere reserve."

You can explore more than 800 miles of car-free forest routes by bike or on horseback, hike along more than 150 miles of well-marked trails, check out rock formations that resemble animals (look for an elephant and a turtle), and, from May to October, rent a kayak or canoe and cruise down the picturesque Loing river, which was often painted by the Impressionists. You can even try rock-climbing and bouldering (rock-climbing without ropes). There are several popular climbs, all classified by color, from white ones just for kids and yellow ones for beginners, all the way up to experts-only black. Just remember to bring water, a map, and something to eat, and have fun getting back to nature, French-style.

MAKE THE MOST OF YOUR TIME Fontainebleau

is 69 kilometers (42 miles) southeast of Paris. By car, take the A6 toll-road to the Fontainebleau exit and then the N7 highway to the town. Several trains run daily from Paris's Gare de Lyon to Fontainebleau-Avon (40 minutes). Take a shuttle bus (June through September only), city bus or taxi to the center of town. At the château, ask for the brochure for kids (*livret-jeux*), which takes them on a treasure hunt. You can tour the gardens by bike or horse-drawn carriage.

FRANCE MINIATURE

If you've ever wished you could visit all of France in a day, now you can. This theme park in a suburb 25 kilometers (16 miles) west of Paris contains more than 150 models of villages, monuments, and other sites from all over France, all carefully re-created at a scale of one-thirtieth the size of the originals. Everything has been done with an attention to detail that can only be described as obsessive.

A reduced version of the real monument's environment surrounds each model, from authentic vegetation right down to the tiniest side street. The real trees and bushes here, 25,000 of them, have been trimmed to one-thirtieth their normal sizes, and the park's landscape designers have made sure that every miniaturized geographical feature represented—every hill, every river—is as accurate as possible. The Château de Versailles surrounded by its gardens looks exactly like the real thing, but smaller, with every turret, fountain, and statue reproduced in a 100-meter (328-foot) display.

MAKE THE MOST OF YOUR TIME
France Miniature is in the village of Élancourt, near St-Quentin-en-Yvelines, which is west of Paris near Versailles. By car, take the A13 highway west of Paris, then the A12 toward St-Quentin-en-Yvelines. Follow the signs to France Miniature. By rail from Paris's Gare Montparnasse, take the train to La Verrière; then follow the signs to the France Miniature bus (#411), which takes you to the park. A combined train-bus-park-entrance ticket for France Miniature is available at Paris train stations.

25 rte. du Mesnil, Élancourt

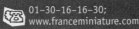 01-30-16-16-30;
www.franceminiature.com

 Sept–June €18.50 ages 15 and up, €12.50 children 4–14; July and Aug €19.50 ages 15 and up, €13.50 children 4–14

 Apr–June, daily 10–6; July–Aug and school holidays daily 10–7; Sept–mid-Nov, W–Th and Sa–Su 10–6

4 and up

It's certainly a little strange to see an Eiffel Tower whose first level you could reach out and touch while standing on the ground (if you were allowed to touch the displays, which you are not), but kids will love running around this Lilliputian world, picking out the monuments they recognize. Animated figures, taped sounds, lakes and rivers, and electronically controlled boats, trains, and cars bring the displays to life. Kids learn something here, too, because the park demonstrates not only France's geography and topography but also the country's great variety of architectural styles, from ancient to modern, as well as regional differences. Special events are regularly organized in the park, and brochures (English versions available) help you take your own tours from particular perspectives. To keep kids entertained, the park has some fun rides, including roller coasters (normal-sized) and even a 30-foot-tall slide that six people can slide down at a time. From on top, you'll feel like you're flying over France.

EATS FOR KIDS

The theme park contains a snack bar and a restaurant, **Les Provinces** (open 12–2), that features typical dishes from various French provinces (quiche with tomatoes and olives from Provence, or grilled goat cheese from the Loire Valley, for example). The park also has a picnic area.

KEEP IN MIND Another attraction nearby (convenient only if you're traveling by car, though) is La Ferme de Gally (route de Bailly, Saint-Cyr-l'École, tel. 01–30–14–60–60, www.gally.com), a working farm where classes (in French) teach kids how to bake bread, plant strawberries, or do other farm tasks (call or check the Web site to get class times, and arrive 45 minutes early to sign up). There's also a path with posted information about flora and fauna of the French countryside, and from late June to October you can get lost in a giant labyrinth cut out of a cornfield.

HALLE SAINT-PIERRE

This is an innovative arts center for kids that the whole family can enjoy. Housed in a beautifully renovated 19th-century structure that was once a covered food market, the Halle Saint-Pierre is just off pretty Willette park, which slopes down the steep hillside under Sacré-Coeur. Among its many offerings, the center has an exhibition space for temporary shows geared to children and families (one celebrated an imaginary country of colorful nature-worshippers); one-hour *ateliers* (workshops) for kids in dance, music, and art; a folk art museum; and other performances and programs of interest to artistically minded kids.

One of the main reasons the Halle Saint-Pierre is popular among Parisian families is the ateliers, which are held all year long on Wednesdays, Saturdays, and during school vacations from 2:30 to 4 (in French). Classes are usually geared to the special exhibits going on in the center at the time, and children are encouraged to show up an hour early to tour the exhibit before coming to class.

EATS FOR KIDS The center's in-house **Café Halle Saint-Pierre** is a popular spot for snacks and drinks. **Pomodoro** (20 rue La Vieuville, tel. 01–42–57–13–55), tucked away on a charming cobbled street, gets consistent raves for its friendly atmosphere, fast service, and outstanding pizza to eat in or take out. For food see also Sacré-Coeur and Montmartre (#3).

MAKE THE MOST OF YOUR TIME The children's ateliers are much in demand, so if your kids are interested in participating in one, it's essential to call ahead to find out what's being offered and reserve a place. If you also have children who are too young for the workshops, you can drop the older ones off and play with the younger ones in the nearby park or take them for a ride on the funicular during the 90-minute atelier.

2 rue Ronsard, 18e. Métro: Anvers

 01–42–58–72–89;
www.hallesaintpierre.org

 Center free; museum
€7.50 adults, €6 children
17 and under, €10 with
kids' class

Sept–July, daily 10–6;
Aug, M–F 12–6

 4 and up; ateliers 6–12

Also in the center, the kid-friendly Musée d'Art Naïf Max Fourny has colorful works of folk art that appeal to even the smallest children. They'll laugh at the big painting of giant crabs pinching people with their huge claws and at the portrait of a troupe of musical monkeys. Guignol puppet shows and theatrical performances for kids (in French) are hosted on Wednesday and Saturday afternoons (hours vary), and special events are organized during Halloween, Christmas, and Easter.

The fun continues just outside the center in the place St-Pierre, a little square with a colorful antique merry-go-round and a kids' play area outfitted with a sandbox and climbing equipment. The funicular train that takes you up to Sacré-Coeur (see #3) begins in this square.

KEEP IN MIND Combine your visit to Hall Saint-Pierre with a tour of Sacré-Coeur and the rest of Montmartre, one of Paris's most picturesque neighborhoods, but be aware that many of the streets here are steep and potentially challenging for younger kids. Also: if you're looking for typical French fabrics, check out the nearby Marché Saint-Pierre (2 rue Charles-Nodier, 01–46–06–92–25, www.marchesaintpierre.com), a five-story store where among other things you'll find fabrics, sheets, towels, and thread. This store is one of many in this lively neighborhood.

HÔTEL NATIONAL DES INVALIDES

46

Topped with the glittering gold dome of the 17th-century Église du Dôme church, Les Invalides (as Parisians call it) originally housed a splendid hospital for invalid soldiers who'd served King Louis XIV. Today, this imposing complex of four elegant pavilions around a huge central courtyard is home to Napoléon's tomb (in the Église du Dôme, commissioned by Louis XIV as a church for visiting aristocracy), the adjoining Église St-Louis-des-Invalides (a smaller, very plain church designed for soldier-patients), and the Musée de l'Armée, devoted to France's long military history.

Kids will enjoy seeing the imposing bloodred tomb of the brilliant, power-hungry soldier who began his career calling himself a man of the people and eventually appointed himself emperor. Forced to abdicate in 1814, Napoléon staged a comeback but was then exiled for good in 1815 after his defeat at Waterloo; he died in 1821. Today, Napoléon lies inside a set of coffins made of mahogany, tin, lead, ebony, and oak. He's not going anywhere.

MAKE THE MOST OF YOUR TIME The Musée de l'Armée organizes a number of special activities for kids (in French). In Visites-Contes (visit-stories), children 7–13 and their families are taken around the collection and told entertaining stories about objects (Wednesdays, Saturdays, and some school holidays at 2:30, €7 adults, €6 children). As part of an Armoiries et Emblèmes (Coats of Arms and Crests) workshop, kids create their own personal crests using medieval symbols and colors. Free *parcours-découvertes* (discovery map) brochures contain games and questions that help families see the collection in new ways. For information on kids' classes, call 01–44–42–51–73 (reservations advised).

Esplanade des Invalides, 7e.
Métro: Latour-Maubourg

 €9 ages 18 and up

 Museum Apr–Sept, daily 10–5:45; Oct–Mar, daily 10–5. Napoléon's tomb daily 10–4:45, longer in summer

01–44–42–37–72, 01–44–42–38–77
museum; www.invalides.org

 6 and up

The Musée de l'Armée (Army Museum) displays a vast collection of kid-pleasing weaponry and other military gear: intricate medieval weapons, richly decorated swords, a suit of armor worn by King Henri II when he was a child, early firearms from the time of Louis XIII, a war outfit once worn by the emperor of China, and, for a touch of the macabre, Napoléon's dog and horse, stuffed, in the section of Napoléon memorabilia. You'll also see plenty of coats-of-arms, flags, and scale models of great battles of the past. The recently modernized Département des Deux Guerres Mondiales (section on World Wars I and II) includes a display that re-creates a scene from the liberation of Paris by Allied troops, as well as exhibits on the Résistance movement (a group resisting German occupation) whose Paris headquarters was the Catacombes (see #61). Kids should enjoy taking a look at some choice pieces from the museum's huge collection of military figurines from the 18th to the 20th century, even though these toy soldiers were not intended for kids.

EATS FOR KIDS

For gourmet takeout, visit a nearby branch of the upscale food group **Lenôtre** (36 av. La-Motte-Piquet, tel. 01–45–55–71–25, see also #51). Try the *tapénade* (olive paste to spread on bread) or any of the irresistible pastries. For food see also Musée Rodin (#20) and Tour Eiffel (#1).

KEEP IN MIND Combine your visit here with a trip to the nearby Musée Rodin (#20) and have lunch in the museum's café overlooking a quiet garden. For another respite from crowds, noise, and traffic, take a stroll through the peaceful Jardin Catherine-Labouré, a public garden that was once the property of a convent. It contains a well-maintained orchard as well as sandboxes and a small kids' play area (entrance at 33 rue de Babylone).

JARDIN D'ACCLIMATATION

Ready for a ride on a dragon? Want to see a puppet show, jump on a giant trampoline, and try out the latest interactive computer technology, all in one park? Then come to the Jardin d'Acclimatation, Paris's oldest children's amusement park, which has been pleasing kids and their families since 1860.

This park is an engaging mix of old and new. The attractions include a little mini-farm where farm animals roam free; a petting zoo that's home to small, cuddly creatures like miniature goats; a hall of mirrors; and a sedate family of bears. Youngsters especially love these classics, which just goes to show that old-fashioned amusements can still have great kid appeal.

Moving into the 20th century, you have your choice of two roller coasters (the aforementioned dragon, for smaller kids, and a bigger, scarier coaster for bigger, fearless kids), a merry-go-round, a tame riverboat ride, very untame bumper cars, a miniature golf course, and lots of innovative things to slide down or climb up. One section of the park is just for

EATS FOR KIDS The park contains snack bars and restaurants, including **Le Pavillon des Oiseaux** (tel. 01–45–02–11–61), popular for Sunday brunch, and **La Terrasse du Jardin** (tel. 01–45–00–14–18) with a cozy fireplace. For food see also Bois de Boulogne (#63) and Musée en Herbe (#24).

MAKE THE MOST OF YOUR TIME The most fun way to arrive at the Jardin d'Acclimatation is to take Le Petit Train from the Porte Maillot (at the edge of the Bois de Boulogne) to the park's entrance. The little steam engine–powered train runs every 20 minutes (June–September 10–7, October–May 10–5:45) on Wednesday, Saturday, and Sunday, and daily during school vacations. A €5.40-per-person round-trip ticket includes park admission. Toddlers haven't been forgotten in this park. There are merry-go-rounds and rides adapted to kids as young as two, and kids over the age of one can stroke a bunny in the petting zoo.

Bois de Boulogne, 16e.
Métro: Porte Maillot, Sablons

 €2.90 ages 3 and up; some attractions extra

May–Sept, daily 10–7; Oct–Apr, daily 10–6; train, circus, puppets W, Sa–Su, and school holidays

01–40–67–98–07,
01–40–67–99–05 Ateliers du Jardin;
www.jardindacclimatation.fr

 9 mths–12 yrs

kids under 10. From mid-May to mid-September, happy kids run around on a big paved space topped by tall fountains in the shape of giant sunflowers that spew water all over everyone (bring bathing suits). Explor@dome (tel. 01–53–64–90–40, www.exploradome.com) within the park (but with separate admission, €5) has hands-on science displays and interactive exhibits, and gives classes (in French, €7) for kids 5–14 or 15 and up in which they might learn how to edit a video (in a one-hour class) or make their own short film (two hours). The Musée en Herbe (see #24) is a special kids' museum. Activities for kids three and up are organized in the Ateliers du Jardin on Wednesdays and Saturdays; recent ones have focused on cooking, perfume, or music.

KEEP IN MIND A quirky, kid-pleasing museum not far away is the Musée de la Contrefaçon (16 rue de la Faisanderie, métro Porte-Dauphine, tel. 01–56–26–14–00, www.unifab.com), which is devoted to counterfeits (specifically, to helping people spot them and to showing why they can be a problem). You'll see about 400 fake versions of familiar brand-name goods—from Barbies to Lego to running shoes—that look almost like the real things, but aren't. The oldest object in the museum is a counterfeit Gallo-Roman amphora (vase) created centuries ago, a gift to the museum from Jacques Cousteau.

JARDIN DE SCULPTURE EN PLEIN AIR

44

Paris's open-air sculpture garden, in a little public park (Jardin Tino Rossi) next to a cobblestone quai on the Seine, is one art display that won't bore kids. Officially it's called the Musée de la Sculpture en Plein Air de la Ville de Paris, but that's an awfully unwieldy name for one of the city's most accessible art venues. Here monumental sculptures created by some of the most famous artists of the 20th century (Brancusi, Zadkine, César, and others) can be touched, climbed on, and generally treated like familiar objects. In fact, the whole point of this museum is that it doesn't feel like a museum at all. You'll find no barriers between you and the sculptures, and in fact no barriers between you and the Seine, so keep a close eye on toddlers.

The little park is long and narrow, with rambling, curving sidewalks kids like to skate or ride bikes on. There are lots of trees, flowers, and park benches, though as in most city parks, you're not supposed to walk or sit on the grass. A big children's play area, with climbing

EATS FOR KIDS You can picnic on a park bench, or cross the river behind Notre-Dame and head for the Île St-Louis, where you can sample Paris's most famous ice cream at **Berthillon** (31 rue St-Louis-en-Île, tel. 01–43–54–31–61). You can get a luscious cone to go or sit down in the shop's tearoom, through the door to the right of the take-out window. Try the *gianduja* (chocolate-hazelnut) ice cream. Yum! **Metamorphosis** (3 quai Montebello, in a barge, tel. 01–43–54–08–08) offers meals and magic shows (see Double Fond #52). For food see also Cathédrale de Notre-Dame-de-Paris (#60), Jardin des Plantes (#42), and Muséum National d'Histoire Naturelle (#18).

Quai St-Bernard, 5e. Métro: Austerlitz

08-92-68-30-00 Office de Tourisme;
www.insecula.com/salle/ms00889.html
or www.paris.fr (Mairie de Paris)

 Free

 Daily 24 hrs

All ages

equipment and slides (covered with 21st-century art: graffiti), has a fence around it so little kids can't sneak out while their parents' backs are turned.

The sculpture garden is a favorite spot among Parisians for a Sunday stroll *en famille*, before or after a visit to the nearby Jardin des Plantes (see #42). Musicians, joggers, and people pushing sleeping babies in strollers also hang out, and several houseboats that have been made into living quarters are docked here permanently. On weekends, you'll often see a group of tango fanatics dancing in a paved area next to the river. A special plus is the spectacular view you'll have of Notre-Dame across the Seine, and you won't have to share it with a zillion tour buses.

KEEP IN MIND
Since this garden is accessible to anyone at any time, unsavory types sometimes hang out here at night. During the day, however, the park is constantly patrolled by guards, who, along with ensuring your safety, ensure the safety of the grass.

MAKE THE MOST OF YOUR TIME
The nearby Institut du Monde Arabe (1 rue des Fossés-St-Bernard, tel. 01-40-51-38-38, www.imarabe. org) is a museum and cultural center that gives kids an introduction to the rich history of the Arab world's art and architecture. Special art classes and concerts for kids are organized regularly. Note the building's shutters—fashioned after a camera lense—that automatically move to filter light at the proper angles throughout the day: they're a high-tech version of the traditional Arab *moucharabiehs* (elaborately carved wooden shutters).

JARDIN DES HALLES

This kid-friendly park in the very center of Paris was created on the spot where the city's central open-air food market, Les Halles, stood for 800 years. That Les Halles, the vibrant and picturesque "belly of Paris," moved to the Paris suburb of Rungis in 1969. Its replacement stretches out in beautifully landscaped sections, with historic Église St-Eustache on its north side. Arched trellises remind Parisian old-timers of the iron arches that rose over the old marketplace, but there the nostalgia stops. This is a very modern park that offers all sorts of attractions for families and kids.

Kids like the waterfall, which they can actually get wet in; a fenced-in grassy area just for toddlers and their families; a giant sculpture of a human head (*L'Écoute*—The Listen—by Henri de Miller) that they can climb on; two well-equipped play areas with climbing equipment; and one of Paris's loveliest merry-go-rounds. The drawback is that unsavory

EATS FOR KIDS **Presto Fresco** (14 rue Montmartre, tel. 01–40–26–83–94) serves top-notch pizzas and homemade pastas. Treat the family to ice cream, pastries, or gourmet take-out at **Stohrer** (51 rue Montorgueil, tel. 01–42–33–38–20), a shop that's been tempting Parisians since 1730.

MAKE THE MOST OF YOUR TIME For chic Paris fashions for the whole family, the hip designer Agnès B.'s original flagship boutiques for women, men, and kids are close by on Rue du Jour, a great shopping street (2 & 6 Rue du Jour, tel. 01–45–08–56–56). Parents (and kids) who like to cook shouldn't miss E. Dehillerin right around the corner (18 and 20 Rue Coquillière, tel. 02–41–26–53–13), which has everything from copper pots to the latest kitchen gadgets and was a favorite of Julia Child.

105 rue Rambuteau, 1er.
Métro: Les Halles

 Free

Daily 24 hrs; Jardin des Enfants
T–Su, hrs vary

01–45–08–07–18; www.paris.fr
(Mairie de Paris)

3–12; Jardin des
Enfants 7–11

characters hang out here, especially at night. The park is very well patrolled, but watch out for pickpockets.

Le Jardin des Enfants des Halles, in the southeast corner of the park, is a recently refurbished kids' park that's usually off limits to parents. Friendly staff members guide kids through the park's different "worlds," including the Monde Sonore (World of Sounds), where they try to identify strange sounds, and the Monde Tropical (Tropical World), where they can get lost in a bamboo forest. Only a limited number of kids are allowed in at a time for the one-hour visit. (On Saturdays from 10 to 1, kids can bring their parents with them.)

The Jardin des Halles also has its own vegetable garden (Parisian school kids are brought here to learn that vegetables actually grow in the ground), as well as the biggest tropical greenhouse (under glass pyramids) built in Europe since the 19th century. All in all, there's something for all ages in this very up-to-date park in the heart of one of Paris's oldest neighborhoods.

KEEP IN MIND If you need to do some gift shopping, the Forum des Halles underground shopping mall has all kinds of boutiques, including a branch of Nature et Découvertes (tel. 01–42–28–42–16) that regularly organizes crafts classes for kids and nature-oriented activities for the whole family. FNAC (tel. 08–25–02–00–20) has books, CDs, batteries, film, and memory cards for digital cameras, and FNAC's ticket office sells tickets to many attractions in Paris. The recently renovated Forum des Images (tel. 01–44–76–63–00) shows films and has a huge collection of films on Paris that you can view on video screens.

JARDIN DES PLANTES

Paris's centuries-old botanical garden first opened to the public in 1650, and from that time on it's been drawing families in search of a little nature in the city. Thousands of flowers and plants that look beautiful year-round border the wide graveled walkways leading from the Seine to the Muséum National d'Histoire Naturelle complex. Sitting on a bench here under the manicured 200-year-old plane trees and watching the world go by is one of Paris's great free pleasures.

Kids can run off steam along the central garden's wide paths, and a fun children's play area (on the garden's western edge, near the rue Cuvier) contains lots of structures to climb on, including a huge jungle-gym contraption that looks like a dinosaur. On the garden's southwestern edge, winding paths to the summit of a hill form a maze; on the eastern edge of the park near the Muséum National d'Histoire Naturelle is the Dodo Manège, a charming merry-go-round that lets little kids ride on models of extinct or endangered animals.

The Jardin des Plantes contains the world's oldest public zoo, La Ménagerie, opened in 1794. Kids can see bears, giraffes, lions, orangutans, dozens of monkeys and birds, a variety

MAKE THE MOST OF YOUR TIME Among the park's glories are its masses of irises blooming in spring and its rose garden with hundreds of varieties of roses blooming in spring and summer. If you want to picnic on a park bench while you're feasting your eyes on the flowers, visit the food markets on the place Monge (Wednesday, Friday, and Sunday mornings) and the rue Mouffetard (daily except Monday). L'Épée de Bois (12 rue de l'Épée-de-Bois, tel. 01–43–31–50–18), near rue Mouffetard, is a toy store specializing in high-quality wooden toys.

57 rue Cuvier, quai St-Bernard, 5e.
Métro: Pl. Monge, Jussieu, Gare d'Austerlitz

01-40-79-30-00 Muséum National d'Histoire
Naturelle, 01-40-79-37-94 Ménagerie;
www.paris.fr Mairie de Paris

 Gardens free; Grande
Serre €5; Ménagerie
€7 ages 17 and up,
€5 children 4–16

 Gardens daily 7:30–8;
Ménagerie Apr–Sept, daily 9–6;
Oct–Mar, daily 9–5

All ages

of snakes, and even a few giant turtles. All the animals look well cared for, but their cages are small. This means kids can get a close-up look at them, but the animals themselves look bored and unhappy. At the Microzoo (for kids 10 and up), within the main zoo, kids can use microscopes to check out microscopic animal life, including all the little creatures that live on a piece of cheese (not recommended just before lunch).

Nature-loving kids like checking out a tree that's supposedly the oldest in Paris, a faux acacia—that's the type of the tree, it's not a fake tree—planted in 1636; it's on the allée de Becquerel. The Grande Serre (Great Greenhouse) nearby, which reopened in spring 2010 after extensive renovation, is so full of exotic hothouse plants gone wild, some dating back hundreds of years, that going inside it is like a trip to the tropics. You can also join the Parisians jogging along the park's outer gravel walks. Where else can you jog in a park that's more than 350 years old?

KEEP IN MIND

Kids *really* interested in plants will like the École de Botanique, which has thousands of rare varieties, including a Corsican pine tree planted here in 1784. The Jardin des Plantes' maze—a kid favorite—is on a hillock near the bees and birds garden, a pretty, sheltered area.

EATS FOR KIDS You'll see several snacks stands near the zoo entrance as well as the **Restaurant de La Ménagerie,** whose specialty is crêpes, inside the zoo. **Breakfast in America** (17 rue des Écoles, tel. 01-43-54-50-28) is one of the only places in Paris where you can get a great American-style breakfast (eggs, bacon, hash-brown potatoes, pancakes, the works) from 8:30 in the morning (to fuel a long day of sightseeing) to 10:30 at night; this is also the place to come if you're homesick for a burger, coleslaw, or a BLT. For food see also Muséum National d'Histoire Naturelle (#18).

JARDIN DES TUILERIES

41

Thanks to its wide gravel walks, placid fountains, lawns—all with *pelouse interdite* (keep off the grass) signs—and carefully manicured flower beds stretching between the Louvre and the place de la Concorde, the Jardin des Tuileries is without a doubt the city's most elegant park. For generations, Parisian families have come here for outings. Parents relax on park benches while kids run around or, best of all, sail little boats on one of the park's ponds. (You rent a boat and a long pole from a stand next to the pond, hope your kids' boat will be one of the ones whose sails catch the wind, and encourage your children to use the pole to prod their craft away from the side of the pond if it gets stuck.)

This formal park had very humble beginnings: in the 15th century it was a quarry for clay that was used in making *tuiles* (roof tiles), the source of the park's name. Marie de Medici had the idea of creating an elegant, Italian-style garden here, and later André Le Nôtre, the great 17th-century garden designer responsible for the park around the Château de Versailles, embellished the park.

KEEP IN MIND

You can rent the little toy sailboats to sail in the fountains on Wednesdays, weekends, and school holidays.

MAKE THE MOST OF YOUR TIME

If you're running out of reading material in English, check out nearby WH Smith's, Paris's largest English-language bookstore (248 rue de Rivoli, tel. 01–44–77–88–99). You'll find many children's books upstairs. Galignani (224 rue de Rivoli, tel. 01–42–60–76–07), founded in 1802, sells books in both English and French, and has a particularly extensive selection of art books. Temporary art exhibits, often on photography and sometimes on themes of interest to kids, are held in the Galerie Nationale du Jeu de Paume (1 pl. de la Concorde, tel. 01–47–03–12–50, www.jeudepaume.org) in the northwest corner of the park.

Between pl. de la Concorde and the Louvre,
1er. Métro: Tuileries, Louvre

 Free

 01–40–20–90–43; www.parisinfo.com
(Office de Tourisme)

 Apr–June and Sept, daily 7:30 AM–9 PM;
July–Aug, daily 7 AM–11 PM; Oct–Mar,
daily 7:30 AM–7:30 PM

 All ages

Today, the Tuileries contains many attractions for kids. They can have fun on climbing equipment or explore sandboxes in spacious, shady kids' play areas—including a brand-new one at the Louvre end of the park—or take a ride on the park's venerable merry-go-round or on one of the sleepy ponies led around in a group. There's also a Guignol puppet theater, special paths for skateboarders and rollerbladers, a trampoline, and even an open-air ice-skating rink in winter. From mid-June through August and at Christmas, an enormous, garish carnival rises on the site, complete with a zillion stands where you can try your luck at various games, a roller-coaster ride, and a huge—*really* huge—Ferris wheel. Kids love it, but it's a good thing Marie de Medici and Le Nôtre aren't around to see this.

EATS FOR KIDS There are **snack bars** and **drinks stands** scattered around the Tuileries. **Café Reale** (tel. 01–42–96–63–03), right in the middle of the park, has good *tartines* (open-face sandwiches), though the service can be slow. You can also come here just for a pastry and sit indoors or out. **Angelina** (226 rue de Rivoli, tel. 01–42–60–82–00), a tearoom founded in 1903, serves to-die-for hot chocolate and excellent (though pricey) pastries; try the Mont Blanc, a chestnut–whipped cream extravaganza. For food see also Musée du Louvre (#26), Musée de l'Orangerie (#29), and Jardins du Palais-Royal (#39).

JARDIN DU LUXEMBOURG

This oh-so-Parisian park, the city's favorite for generations, has it all: a beautiful palace, designed in 1615 and now the home of the French Sénat; huge trees; ponies to ride; tennis courts; beehives; the Grand Bassin pond, where kids can sail boats; and even— rarest of all in Paris—an area where you can actually walk on the grass (if you're accompanied by a toddler). One of the park's treasures is its merry-go-round, whose much-loved wooden animals were designed by none other than Charles Garnier, the 19th-century architect of the Opéra de Paris–Garnier (#17). Kids can try to catch a brass ring with a stick. Next to the merry-go-round is the park's own puppet theater, the city's biggest (see Marionnettes du Luxembourg, #36).

You'll find a special fenced-in kids' play area with its own admission charge in the southwest corner of the park, next to the puppet theater. It's kept spotlessly clean (not always the case in Paris parks) and filled with all sorts of play equipment kids can climb on, swing down, swirl through the air on, or simply sit in. Toddlers head to the train or the sandbox,

EATS FOR KIDS **La Buvette des Marionnettes du Luxembourg** next to the puppet theater (tel. 01–43–26–33–04) serves drinks, sandwiches, salads, and snacks, and there are tables outside. To shop for a park-bench picnic, try the famous *patisserie-traiteur* (bakery and take-out shop). **Géard Mulot** (76 rue de Seine, 01–43–26–85–77), for all kinds of delicacies, sweet and savory. **Amorino**, a high-quality chain of gelato shops, has an outpost nearby on Rue Vavin (4 rue Vavin, 01–42–22–66–86). **Bread and Roses** (7 rue Fleurus, tel. 01–43–26–91–13) serves excellent gourmet pizzas, sandwiches, quiches, and salads. The desserts are so good it's almost impossible to choose.

Entrances: rue de Medicis, rue Guynemer, bd. St-Michel, rue de Vaugirard, 6e. Métro: Odéon. RER: Luxembourg

 Free, some attractions charge

 Apr–Oct, daily 7–sunset; Nov–Mar, daily 8–sunset

08–92–68–30–30 Office de Tourisme; www.parisinfo.com; www.paris.fr de Paris

All ages

and bigger kids with an urge to climb gravitate toward the tall slides and a tall spiderweb contraption made of rope that looks a little like the Eiffel Tower.

Chess players congregate in front of the glass-walled Orangerie, which has a free play area for small children in front of it. In the middle of the park, you'll find some placid ponies that take little kids for a short ride. Children in the mood for more action like the pedal-powered cars that operate near the park's southern edge. You can join the joggers along a popular circuit around the park, toss bits of baguette to resident pigeons, or, best of all, sit down in one of the park's distinctive pale-green metal chairs, listen to Parisians (and others) chattering around you, and realize you're really, truly in Paris.

KEEP IN MIND

Perpendicular to the park not far from the playground is **Rue Vavin**, Paris's top shopping street for stylish kid's clothes, shoes, and toys. As Paris is known for some of the finest children's fashions on the planet, it's worth a stroll. Kids and parents alike will love **Jean-Paul Héin**, a top *chocolatier* (3 rue Vavin, 01–43–54–09–85).

MAKE THE MOST OF YOUR TIME

Fans of Little Nemo would enjoy visiting his clown-fish relatives at the nearby Centre de la Mer (195 rue St-Jacques, tel. 01–44–32–10–70, www.oceano.org). This museum/aquarium complex is designed to make people—especially kids—more sensitive to aquatic life forms. Exhibits, many of them interactive, are accessible even to very young children. Classes for kids 3–8 let them touch various sea creatures, and a treasure hunt (in French) for kids 8–12 is popular among Parisian kids (tel. 01–44–32–10–95 to reserve a spot in a class or treasure hunt; €3 for either activity).

JARDINS DU PALAIS-ROYAL

The Jardins du Palais-Royal (actually a single park, although the name is plural) is one of Paris's best-kept secrets, even though it's right in the middle of the most touristed part of the city, just a short walk from the Louvre. Often overlooked by visitors, this lovely little park surrounded by elegant 18th-century buildings (the writer Colette lived in one of them) is hard to find. You get to it by going through small passageways that you could walk right past and not see.

The park has long gravel walkways, manicured trees, magnificently planted flower beds, lots of park benches, and—most special of all—hardly any traffic noise, because the palace buildings surrounding it block out the sound of the cars roaring by just a few yards away. Although it looks very formal, the park is popular among Parisian families, especially ones with smaller kids, since they can run around safe from traffic.

EATS FOR KIDS **A Priori Thé** (35–37 Galerie Vivienne, 66 rue Vivienne, tel. 01–42–97–48–75) is a tearoom with American-style treats under the glass roof of the Galerie Vivienne. **Paul** (25 av. de l'Opéra, tel. 01–42–60–78–22), a popular bakery chain, has sandwiches, salads, and pastries. For food also see Jardin des Tuileries (#41) and Musée du Louvre (#26).

MAKE THE MOST OF YOUR TIME Near Palais-Royal is Paris's most exclusive (and expensive) cooking school, the Ritz hotel's École Ritz-Escoffier (38 rue Cambon, tel. 01–43–16–30–50, www.ritzparis.com), which has classes for adults; for kids 6–11, "Ritz Kids"; or for ages 12–16 "Toques Junior." The 2½-hour classes (in French, but teachers speak English) are held on Wednesdays twice a month. Each class teaches kids how to prepare a special treat (like canapés or *macarons*). Students wear chef's jackets with the Ritz hotel logo, and sometimes get to visit the hotel's kitchens after the class. They also get a souvenir photo, but there's a catch: each class costs €95.

Entrances: off pl. André-Malraux, rue Beaujolais, rue de Valois, 1er. Métro: Palais-Royal

 Free

Apr–May and Sept, daily 7:30 AM–9:30 PM; June–Aug, daily 7 AM–11 PM; Oct–Mar, daily 7:30 AM–8:30 PM

 All ages

08–92–68–30–30 Office de Tourisme; www.parisinfo.com; www.paris.fr

Toddlers can practice taking steps from park bench to park bench or play in the sandbox at the north end of the park, while bigger kids can kick a soccer ball or just play around on the artwork and fountain at the south end of the park. One of these, an installation by architect Daniel Buren, caused a controversy when it was built—its contemporary style contrasts sharply with the 18th-century structures around it—but kids love it. The newly renovated installation is a wide expanse of pavement with water flowing under it, visible through grids. Punctuating it are a series of columns kids can climb on and rows of little red lights in the pavement that make it look like a miniature landing strip. Don't forget to toss a coin into the pool near the columns and make a wish—it's a Paris tradition. Among the other public art here is a fountain with shiny silver balls, created by Pol Bury. In a flat, paved area around the fountain, little kids practice their roller-skating skills and supremely talented skateboarders sometimes show off their stuff. Kids might not know it's art, but they know they like it.

KEEP IN MIND After enjoying this peaceful park, you could indulge in some window-shopping under the elegant arcades. Along with some top names in fashion, there are several boutiques kids will enjoy. At the jewel-like Boîtes à Musique Anna Joliet a dazzling array of music boxes can be personalized with dozens of songs. Across the way, the favorite French toy shop Vilac has a tempting selection of dolls, puzzles and classic wooden toys. You'll also find chic shops on the faubourg St-Honoré. Bonpoint (320 rue St-Honoré, 01–49–27–94–82) has gorgeous, oh-so-Parisian (and oh-so-pricey) clothes for babies and kids.

LES ARTS DÉCORATIFS

Les Arts Décoratifs (The Decorative Arts), an associated group of organizations housed in the Marsan wing of the Louvre, reopened to great fanfare in 2006 after a 10-year renovation project. The result: outstanding displays in three kid-friendly museums on the premises.

The vast Musée des Arts Décoratifs (Museum of Decorative Arts) shows you how French people's tastes in decoration have changed over the years and how these tastes reflect social and political realities. Big hits for kids are the period rooms—re-creations of typical rooms from the Middle Ages to the early 20th century—that let you see how French people (the wealthy ones) actually lived back then.

Check out the 15th-century bedroom, with its very short bed covered with pillows; people slept almost sitting up back then, as lying all the way down was associated with death. An 18th-century salon from a private mansion has fragile, carefully arranged chairs, rich drapes, a golden harp, and other precious objects. A favorite among children is the Galerie de Jouets (toy gallery) with more than 12,000 toys, while the Galerie des Bijoux (jewelry

EATS FOR KIDS The Musée des Arts Décoratifs has an elegant restaurant, **Le Saut du Loup**, that serves lunch or weekend brunch on a beautiful outdoor terrace in the Louvre gardens: it's worth it for the Paris views alone, but the food is great, too. It's also the perfect spot for afternoon tea, €6. **Le Pain Quotidien** (18 pl. du Marché-St-Honoré, tel. 01–42–96–31–70) is a branch of the Belgian chain that's taken Paris (and the rest of the world) by storm. Salads, open-face sandwiches, and a daily special are served at lunch. For food see also Musée du Louvre (#26), Jardin des Tuileries (#41), Jardins du Palais-Royal (#39), and Musée de l'Orangerie (#29).

107 rue de Rivoli, 1er.
Métro: Palais-Royal, Louvre, Tuileries

 €9 ages 18 and up,
workshops €120–€160

01–44–55–57–50;
www.lesartsdecoratifs.fr

T–W and F 11–6, Th 11–9,
Sa–Su 10–6

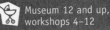 Museum 12 and up,
workshops 4–12

gallery), displaying jewelry from the Middle Ages to today, should delight all fans of pretty objects.

In the main exhibit hall of the Musée de la Publicité (Museum of Advertising), you can check out choice pieces from the museum's collection of some 100,000 posters from the 18th century to the present. Exhibits change every six months, so you might see a 1744 Paris playbill one visit or gorgeous posters designed by Toulouse-Lautrec on another. You can also use the video screens to see the museum's collection of ads, posters, and TV commercials.

Fashion-loving kids and teens will like the Musée de la Mode et du Textile (Museum of Fashion and Textiles), which showcases clothes that have been in style from 1700 to today, from corsets to miniskirts. Exhibits change regularly, but you might see the wardrobe of an 18th-century lady, creations by Yves Saint-Laurent, heavily brocaded vests worn by Parisian men during the French revolution, or the latest fashions from today's designers.

KEEP IN MIND

Excellent temporary exhibits have included depictions of animals large, small, and imaginary in a child's world; a comprehensive two-part exhibition retracing the history of contemporary fashion; and another on the color red. Ninety-minute guided tours for families (in French, but most guides speak English) are given on weekends (tel. 01–44–55–59–25 for reservations).

MAKE THE MOST OF YOUR TIME

The Musée des Arts Décoratifs runs two- to three-hour workshops (in French) for kids 6–18, divided into groups according to age. Workshops begin with a tour of the collections (for younger kids, this is in the form of a treasure hunt), followed by a hands-on session in which children can create something. They might make a decorative object in medieval style, design a poster or comic book, or make their own jewelry. The workshops are held on Wednesdays and school holidays (tel. 01–44–55–59–25 to make reservations).

LES ÉGOUTS

37

Come to Paris and tour the sewers? Yuck! Well, that might be your reaction, but kids seem to be enthusiastic about visiting the city's collective plumbing system. And they're not the only ones; Paris's sewer tour has become so popular that lines for it can get really long in summer. The tour's appeal seems to lie in seeing Paris's flip side: the dark, smelly underbelly of the gleaming, elegant city overhead. Don't worry; you won't have to walk in or touch anything icky.

You visit a small underground museum and an area where you pick up a brochure (English version available) and see a film (in French) on Paris's public sanitation system, from its earliest days to the present. Next, you go on a tour of the sewers in action. Guides take groups through a few well-lit tunnels to show you how the system works (tours in English offered in summer). Each tunnel is marked with the name of the street it serves, and pipes coming from individual buildings are marked with their addresses. As in the Catacombes

KEEP IN MIND You could combine a visit to Les Égouts with a trip to the Tour Eiffel, if the lines aren't too long. If your group needs some fresh air after the sewer tour, Champ-de-Mars park, just under the tower, with its open spaces and kids' play areas, is just a short stroll away.

EATS FOR KIDS **Thoumieux** (79 rue St-Dominique, tel. 01–47–05–49–75), a classic bistro owned by the same family for three generations, prepares homey French dishes at very reasonable prices. With authentic turn-of-the-20th-century decor, **Secco** (20 rue Jean-Nicot, tel. 01–47–05–80–88) is famous for its sourdough baguettes, *cannelés* (soft, yeast-risen sweet cakes), and freshly made sandwiches. Treat yourself to sublime chocolates made on the premises from **Michel Chaudun** (149 rue de l'Université, tel. 01–47–53–74–40); the pistachio chocolate truffles are out of this world. For food see also Palais de Chaillot (#15) and Tour Eiffel (#1).

93 quai d'Orsay, 7e.
Métro: Alma-Marceau

 01-53-68-27-81;
www.parisinfo.com

 €4.30 ages 17 and up,
€3.50 ages 5-16

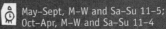 May-Sept, M-W and Sa-Su 11-5;
Oct-Apr, M-W and Sa-Su 11-4

 10 and up

(see #61), across town, you'll discover that there's a whole world under your feet wherever you go in Paris.

Along the way, you'll discover that sewers are a fairly recent innovation for Paris. Up until the Middle Ages, the city got its drinking water from the Seine and disposed of its waste in surrounding fields or by piping garbage and other refuse through narrow, open channels of packed earth called *ruelles* (a name many small streets still have). Around 1200, King Philippe-Auguste had many Parisian streets paved, with channels running down their middles to carry waste away. During Napoléon's time, underground sewers with arched ceilings were installed, but it wasn't until the 1850s, when Baron Haussmann overhauled the whole city by laying huge boulevards through it, that today's extensive sewer system began to take form. It's mind-boggling to think of how the city must have smelled until that time. You'll get a hint of it from the strong, *je ne sais quoi* smell permeating your tour.

MAKE THE MOST OF YOUR TIME The tour takes
an hour (not counting the time spent standing in line to get in), and people with claustrophobic tendencies may be uncomfortable. While you're in the neighborhood, you might want to visit Paris's Église Américaine (American Church; 65 quai d'Orsay, tel. 01-47-05-07-99). In addition to services, the church sponsors or hosts a number of public-service organizations, language classes, and activities for children and families. A bulletin board near the main desk has notices about activities and other subjects of interest to Paris's expat American community.

MARIONNETTES DU LUXEMBOURG

Puppet theaters abound in Paris, but the city's largest is excellently located in the lovely Jardin du Luxembourg (#40). It's the Marionnettes du Luxembourg, and the classic puppet shows staged here are bound to please your kids whether they speak French or not.

Opened in 1933, the puppet theater occupies a nondescript building in the middle of the park, next to the merry-go-round and near the fenced-in play area. Before each show, staff members ring a bell outside the theater to let you know it's time to stand in line.

The shows change regularly, but all feature the classic French puppet hero Guignol, who has been around since at least the 18th century, when he was cast as a bloodthirsty villain. Today, Guignol is definitely the good guy. He's the character with a black pigtail wearing a long Chinese-style coat, but you won't have to look for him, because as soon as he appears on stage every French kid in the audience will shriek his name. Guignol has a good heart but is constantly getting into trouble, usually by trying to help out one of his neighbors

EATS FOR KIDS **La Buvette des Marionnettes du Luxembourg** (tel. 01–43–26–33–04), next to the theater, has drinks, snacks, and light meals. **Pierre Hermé** (72 rue Bonaparte, tel. 01–43–54–47–77) isn't considered the top pastry chef in Paris for nothing: his *mille-feuilles* are perfection and the *macarons* (light, meringue-ish cookies) are legendary. **La Crêperie des Canettes** (10 rue des Canettes, tel. 01–43–26–27–65) has yummy *galettes* (main-dish crêpes) and dessert crêpes. Take a stroll to Paris's famous bakery, **Poîlane**, where kids will love the apple tarts (8 rue du Cherche-Midi, tel. 01–45–48–42–59). For food see also Jardin du Luxembourg (#40).

Jardin du Luxembourg, 6e.
Métro: Odéon. RER: Luxembourg

01–43–26–46–47;
www.paris.fr Mairie de Paris

€4.50

W, Sa–Su, and school holidays
at 3 and 5 (sometimes 2 shows)

4 and up

in the generic French village (or Paris neighborhood) where he lives. As Guignol stumbles blindly into one disaster after another, kids scream advice to him, warn him about the bad guys, and in general try to help him, but no matter what they do, Guignol is bound to get his head whacked more than once. Your children should have no problem getting the gist of the story. Unfortunately, the dialogues at this puppet theater are prerecorded, but kids don't seem to mind. At intermission, the curtain closes and kids crowd around the front of the stage, where nice ladies sell candy.

Guignol always manages to emerge unscathed, and at the end of each show, he takes a few bows and tells the audience to come back again soon. Your kids will no doubt be happy to do just that.

MAKE THE MOST OF YOUR TIME A
few minutes' walk away is Tea and Tattered Pages (24 rue Mayet, tel. 01–40–65–94–35), one of Paris's best sources for used books in English. It's also a cozy tearoom.

KEEP IN MIND Other good Parisian puppet theaters are the Guignol du Jardin d'Acclimatation, in the Bois de Boulogne (16e); the Marionnettes du Champ-de-Mars, near the Eiffel Tower (7e); the Marionnettes des Champs-Élysées, in the Jardin des Champs-Élysées (8e); the Guignol de Paris, in the Parc des Buttes Chaumont (19e); and the Marionnettes du Parc Georges Brassens (15e). Performances at all of them are given on Wednesday, Saturday, and Sunday afternoons and more often during school vacations.

MÉDAILLONS D'ARAGO

35

Paris is filled with monuments to France's native sons and daughters, but there's one you could easily miss. In fact, you could step on it and not see it, and finding it is a treasure hunt kids should enjoy. The monument honors Dominique Arago (1786–1853), an astronomer and physicist who made major contributions to the early study of electromagnetism and who patriotically championed the Paris meridian (the longitude line that passes through the city) as the international mean-time line. France and Ireland actually kept to French mean time until 1911, when both countries joined the world in adopting Greenwich mean time.

In honor of Arago's achievements, France erected a bronze statue of him that once stood on the boulevard Arago (also named for him), but the German army melted the statue down during World War II. In 1995 Arago was again honored, this time with a most unusual monument, conceived by Dutch artist Jan Dibbits: a series of 135 bronze *médaillons* (disks)— each 12 centimeters (4½ inches) in diameter and marked simply with the name Arago—

KEEP IN MIND The detailed Institut Géographique National (IGN) map of Paris, sold at most Paris bookstores and newspaper shops, shows the meridian line. Hint: While several of the Arago disks have been stolen, there are at least three set in the floor in the ground-floor French sculpture section of the Musée du Louvre's Richelieu wing.

MAKE THE MOST OF YOUR TIME The Observatoire de Paris (61 av. de l'Observatoire, tel. 01–40–51–23–97, www.obspm.fr), where Arago once worked, has been a center for the study of time and the stars since it was built in 1667. Its south wall is on Paris's latitude line (48°50′), and the Paris meridian passes right through it. You can take a guided tour (in French) on Tuesday and Thursday at 2 (advance reservations necessary). Kids should enjoy seeing the *horloges parlantes* (talking clocks), the room with a band of bronze marking the meridian line, the 19th-century telescopes, and the various astronomers' tools.

Sq. Île-de-Seine, 98 bd. Arago (14e) to Montmartre
library, 18 av. Pte-de-Montmartre (18e).
Métro: Denfert-Rochereau, St-Jacques

Free

Daily 24 hrs

08–92–68–30–30 Office de Tourisme;
www.parisinfo.com

4 and up

implanted in the pavement along the Paris meridian line. The line of disks (some of which have been stolen) begins where Arago's statue once stood, on the boulevard Arago facing the gardens of the Observatoire de Paris (Paris Observatory).

The line of Arago disks passes through the Jardin du Luxembourg (#40) and the Jardins du Palais-Royal (#39) before ending on the city's northern edge, in front of the Bibliothèque de la Porte de Montmartre (Montmartre's public library). In 2000, a project was launched to plant trees (sometimes accompanied by bronze disks) along the French meridian line all the way from Barcelona to Dunkirk, and now you'll find bronze disks marked *L'An 2000— La Méridienne Verte* (Year 2000—The Green Meridian) near some of the Arago disks in Paris. France's meridian, though invisible, is clearly still alive and well. To go on a treasure hunt, start anywhere along the Paris meridian, and look out for Arago under your feet.

EATS FOR KIDS Nearby Rue Daguerre is one of Paris's liveliest market streets, with a vendor for every French delicacy imaginable. You'll find the freshest seasonal fruits and vegetables, cheeses, biodynamic wines, charcuterie, seafood, and much more, interspersed with some great boutiques. For a quick bite, **Enzo** pizzeria is the place. Consistently on Paris's top-10 best lists of pizza places, this one stands out for its gastronomic pizzas, pastas, and generous salads.

MUSÉE CARNAVALET, HISTOIRE DE PARIS

34

Of all Paris's museums, this one stands out because it's the only one that focuses on the city itself. Paris's long history, from prehistoric times through the 20th century, is brought to life through paintings, sculpture, furnishings, crafts, signs, and everyday objects, all imaginatively presented in two gorgeous adjoining 16th–17th century town houses in the heart of the Marais district.

The sheer variety of things on display here is bound to spark imaginations. Top choices for children include the wooden canoes used by prehistoric fishermen on the Seine and the Salle des Enseignes (Signs Room) with its colorful shopkeeper's signs from Paris at the turn of the 20th century; there's a sign for a *fromagerie* (cheese store) that features three satisfied-looking mice. In the rooms focusing on Paris in the 17th century, take a look at the painting *Le Louvre vu du Pont-Neuf* (The Louvre Seen from the Pont Neuf), which shows you just how vivid (and unrestrained) street life in Paris was in those days. The museum also has

EATS FOR KIDS There are tearooms, wine bars, and food shops throughout the Marais, but for a special treat, have a meal at **Café des Musées** (49, rue de Turenne, tel. 01–42–72–96–17), a neighborhood bistro where you can sample foie gras (duck or goose liver), house-smoked organic salmon, and fries that some say are the best in Paris. The fixed-price menu at lunch is a good deal. **Pozzetto** (39 rue du Roi de Sicile, tel. 01–42–77–08–64) is a gelato-lovers paradise. Their to-die-for gianduja (chocolate-hazelnut) and pistacchio du Roi de Sicile are made from only the best natural ingredients. For food see also Musée Picasso (#21), Place des Vosges and the Marais (#6), and Musée d'Art et d'Histoire du Judaïsme (#33).

23 rue de Sévigné, 3e.
Métro: Chemin Vert or Saint-Paul

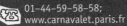

01-44-59-58-58;
www.carnavalet.paris.fr

Permanent exhibits free,
€8 temporary shows

4 and up

many replicas of typical rooms of different periods, including Marcel Proust's bedroom, to show you just how Parisians of the past really lived.

In the rooms devoted to the French Revolution, kids can check out a guillotine and a chess set Louis XVI played with before losing his head, or a model of Bastille prison before the revolutionaries tore it down—an act now celebrated on July 14, France's independence day. Other displays range from Napoléon's cradle to pictures showing the Tour Eiffel under construction. The museum organizes various workshops for kids 4–12, including ones in which they re-create a mosaic like those found on the floors of private homes in Gallo-Roman Paris, or try their hand at producing their own wooden inlays like those on pieces of furniture in the museum, among other choices. A special drawing course for children with hearing problems is also offered. Paris's very own museum definitely does the city proud.

KEEP IN MIND

You could easily devote a day (or more) to the Marais district (see Place des Vosges and the Marais, #6) and its exceptional museums. Be sure to take the time to stroll around this vibrant, beautiful neighborhood and enjoy its many small parks, historic buildings, and tempting shops.

MAKE THE MOST OF YOUR TIME

The two-hour workshops for kids (€6.50), held on Wednesdays and Saturdays, are divided into ones for kids 4–6, 7–9, or 10–12, except for one that teaches kids 10 and up how to create an engraving. Several story hours are also organized regularly (€3.80). All activities are in French, but most staff members speak English. Reserve in advance.

MUSÉE D'ART ET D'HISTOIRE DU JUDAÏSME

33

This innovative museum, housed in a beautiful 17th-century mansion, traces the history of Jewish art and culture in France (as well as elsewhere in Europe and in North Africa). The collection takes you from the Middle Ages (in a display of medieval religious objects and tomb decorations discovered in the Latin Quarter) to modern times, including paintings by Marc Chagall, Modigliani, and Michel Kikoïne that illustrate the importance of Jewish artists to contemporary art history.

Events that have especially marked the history of the Jewish people in France, including the Dreyfus case and the persecution of Jews during World War II (in the "To Be a Jew in Paris in 1939" exhibit) are treated in depth. The museum's rich permanent collection includes images, furnishings, art works, films, and religious objects (menorahs, Torah ornaments and ark curtains, in both the Ashkenazi and Sephardim traditions).

This museum aims to make its collection accessible to families and kids by offering guided family tours, story hours, and very creative workshops. A recent workshop for kids 4–

KEEP IN MIND The Mémorial de la Shoah (17 rue Geoffroy-d'Asnier, 4e, tel. 01–42–77–44–72, www.memorialdelashoah.org) is a museum/cultural center. Its Wall of Names lists the names of 76,000 Jewish people, including 11,000 children, who were deported from France during the war. Only around 2,500 of them survived.

EATS FOR KIDS The Marais has been Paris's Jewish neighborhood for centuries, and though many of the kosher shops have been replaced by fashion boutiques, you can still find traditional treats. Check out **Chez Marianne** (2 rue des Hospitalières-Saint-Gervais, tel. 01–42–72–18–86), famous for its falafel and other goodies. **Finkelsztajn** (27 rue des Rosiers, tel. 01–42–72–78–91) has irresistible pastries, breads, and snacks; try the smoky eggplant dip. **L'As du Falafel** (34 rue des Rosiers, tel. 01–48–87–63–60) serves their bountiful falafel sandwiches to go, from a window in front, or you can sit at a table and be served. Lines can be long but move fast.

71 rue du Temple, 3e.
Métro: Rambuteau or Hôtel de Ville

€6.80 adults 27 and older,
€4.50 ages 18–26

M–F 11–6, Su 10–6, closed for
certain religious holidays

01–53–01–86–60;
www.mahj.org

8 and up

7 focused on Noah's ark and encouraged kids to find images of animals in works in the museum's collection. Recent workshops for kids 8–12 included Tous sous le Même Ciel (Everyone under the Same Sky), in which kids compared stories of Abraham in the Jewish, Christian, and Islamic religions. Workshops for families with kids 5 and up have included ones on Jewish lullabies and on cooking for the Sabbath.

This museum also shows films related to Jewish art and history, organizes conferences and other events, and is known for its creative temporary exhibits, like a recent one that showed how important Jewish writers and artists have been to the history of comic books. Kids of all ages are sure to find something to interest them here, and will come away having learned something about the major contributions Jewish people have made to French culture.

MAKE THE MOST OF YOUR TIME Call or check

the Web site for upcoming workshops, guided tours, story hours, and other events that will be offered during your visit, and to reserve a spot in the workshops (tel. 01–53–01–86–62). All activities are in French but most staff members can speak English. Workshops for kids last around two hours and are held on Wednesdays, Sundays, and school holidays; films and guided tours are usually offered on Sundays.

MUSÉE DE LA MAGIE ET MUSÉE DES AUTOMATES

Any kid (or grown-up) who has ever tried to perform magic tricks is bound to be enthralled by this very unusual museum housed in 16th-century vaulted cellars in the heart of the ancient Marais district. Visitors set out on a journey into the world of illusion, their senses on the alert as they try to separate truth from falsehood. It's not easy. You see strange animated objects, test your perceptions with interactive optical illusions, learn the secrets of bizarre scientific equipment, and check out various tools of the magician's trade. And the really original feature of this museum is that staff members perform magic tricks throughout your visit to show you the magician's craft in action.

This is museum as performance space, and audience participation is part of the show. You see conjuring tricks, sleight-of-hand card tricks, and other thought-teasers that have attracted audiences to magic shows for centuries. The museum's exhibits also give you a history of magic from ancient times to the present. Everything is in French, but staff members are usually able to make explanations in English, if necessary; gestures can go a long way,

MAKE THE MOST OF YOUR TIME The École de Magie is a popular family activity, so it's best to check opening times and reserve in advance if you'd like to participate. After your visit to the museum, you might want to take a look at the nearby Magasin de Magie store (13 rue du Temple, tel. 01–42–74–06–74, www.magasindemagie.com), where you can stock up on magic wands, boxes with secret compartments, decks of trick cards, and even videos (in French) showing you how to perform various magic tricks.

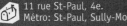
11 rue St-Paul, 4e.
Métro: St-Paul, Sully-Morland

Museum €9 ages 13 and up, €7 children 3–12; École de Magie €20; €6 ages 13 and up, €5 ages 3–12

W, Sa–Su, and school holidays, 10–7

01–42–72–13–26; www.museedelamagie.com

Museum 6 and up, magic classes 12 and up

too. The enthusiastic guides are very good at getting kids involved in the act and try to give every child a chance to participate at some point. You're also given time to conduct your own experiments with the interactive equipment.

The museum also operates the École de Magie (School of Magic), open to anyone 12 or older, adults included, with separate classes for advanced students (2–3 PM) and beginners (3–4:15 PM). All classes are in French, but most instructors speak English. The whole family can learn how to wow friends back home with feats of illusion. Kids also love the Musée des Automates (within the main museum but with separate admission), where they can check out more than 100 rare automated figures that they can manipulate with interactive tools. It's magic.

KEEP IN MIND
For more magic entertainment, check out Double Fond café-theater (#52), where everything, including your disappearing drink, is done by sleight-of-hand, and the Metamorphosis Theatre de Magie de Paris (#52 Keep In Mind), a theater-restaurant in a houseboat on the Seine.

EATS FOR KIDS Le Loir Dans La Théière (3 rue des Rosiers, tel. 01–42–72–90–61), a tearoom, serves scrumptious snacks in a comfy, casual setting. The Marais branch of **Breakfast in America** (7 rue Malher, tel. 01–42–72–40–21) serves delicious American-style breakfast and other familiar treats all day long. For picnic goods, check out the food shops on the rue St-Antoine. For food also see Double Fond (#52) and Place des Vosges and the Marais (#6).

MUSÉE DE LA POUPÉE

The doll lovers in your family won't want to miss this small museum. Hidden away on a tiny dead-end street and with a minuscule front garden, the museum is the perfect home for the more than 500 dolls on display, most of them produced in France from 1800 to 2000. You'll see examples of all sorts of dolls made out of all sorts of materials, from porcelain and papier-mâché to rubber and plastic.

Beyond the displays of dolls, this museum gives you a history of the doll in France since the beginning of the 19th century. From 1800 to 1870, for example, French dolls represented women and came complete with elaborate outfits that would put Barbie to shame, but a doll exhibit at the Paris world's fair of 1878 started a new trend of dolls in the form of babies and kids. From playing with dolls meant to look like *maman* (mom), little French girls began to play at being maman themselves, and the museum's collection shows you this evolution in hundreds of examples.

KEEP IN MIND Bleuette, an early-20th-century equivalent of Barbie, came with a lot more clothes than most kids have in their closets. Very industrious owners could sew more outfits for Bleuette using patterns. The Bleuette displays show kids what girls had to wear a century ago.

MAKE THE MOST OF YOUR TIME The dead-end street on which the museum is located is tricky to find; it begins near 22 rue Beaubourg. This museum would make a good side trip on the day you visit the nearby Centre National d'Art et de Culture Georges Pompidou (#59). If your family has divided opinions on doll museums, some of you—accompanied by a parent—can run around on the square in front of the Pompidou center or check out the Tinguely–Saint-Phalle fountain while others visit the Musée de la Poupée.

Impasse Berthaud, 3e.
Métro: Rambuteau

01-42-72-73-11;
www.museedelapoupeeparis.com

 €8 adults, €5 ages 12–25,
€3 children 3–11; guided
tour or story hr, €13 adults,
€10 ages 12–25,
€8 children 3–11

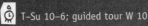 T-Su 10–6; guided tour W 10

 3 and up

The elaborate settings in which the dolls are presented provide a visual overview of fashions and domestic life in France since the early 19th century and should interest even non-doll-fans. Fashion lovers can check out what a well-dressed Parisienne would have been wearing around 1810, see a variety of regional costumes, and get a close look at 1950s styles through several dolls that a French fashion magazine originally sold. Younger kids should enjoy seeing the kinds of clothes children once wore and the tiny toys in several displays that show what French kids have played with over the years. Reserve in advance to take a guided tour of the collection (in French).

The Musée de la Poupée includes a doll hospital where you can bring dolls to be repaired; collectors can purchase rare (and very expensive) dolls as well as parts to be used in restoring antique dolls. At the museum's small shop, you can buy dolls, doll clothes, and doll furniture. Don't miss the tiny copper pans that no French doll kitchen should ever be without.

EATS FOR KIDS Tiny **Le Potager du Marais** (22 rue Rambuteau, tel. 01–42–74–24–66), around the corner from the doll museum, prepares tasty vegetarian dishes made with organic ingredients. You'll find soups, salads, quiches, eggplant dip, and other special treats; reservations recommended. It's very popular so it's likely you'll be practically elbow-to-elbow with other diners. For food see also Centre National d'Art et de Culture Georges Pompidou (#59), Musée Picasso (#21), Musée d'Art et d'Histoire du Judaïsme (#33), and Musée des Arts et Métiers (#28).

MUSÉE DE L'AIR ET DE L'ESPACE

For anyone who loves airplanes, this air and space museum is a must. It's in the historic Aéroport Le Bourget, the former main city airport. If the name sounds familiar, that's because aviator Charles Lindbergh landed his *Spirit of St. Louis* here in May 1927, becoming the first person to complete a transatlantic flight. What you may not know is that 13 days earlier, pilots Charles Nungesser and François Coli took off from Le Bourget in an attempt to do the same—but disappeared. You can learn about their flight and other aviation history at this vast exhibition space, which occupies the former main terminal and part of a runway, and showcases air travel (and dreams of it) from 1500 to the present.

The Prototypes 1945–1970 et l'Armée de l'Air exhibit contains prototypes and military aircraft, and Entre Deux Guerres displays light aircraft and stunt planes from 1920 to 1970, with a concentration on nonmilitary aircraft from the 1920s and 1930s (the period between the two world wars that the exhibit name implies). The Hall de l'Espace has models of satellites, including *Sputnik 57*, and of *Apollo 13*, and in the Hall Concorde you can climb aboard the prototype for the first Concorde and see famous planes flown during World War II, such as

MAKE THE MOST OF YOUR TIME
To get here by car or taxi, take the A1 highway north of Paris to the Aérogare Le Bourget exit (around 8 kilometers/5 miles). By public transport, take the métro to La Courneuve–8 Mai stop, or take the RER commuter train (line B) from central Paris to Le Bourget, which is a stop on the train to Aéroport Roissy–Charles-de-Gaulle. From outside the entrance of either the métro or the RER station, take the number 152 bus to Aérogare Le Bourget. The trip by public transportation should take around 30 minutes, depending on train and bus connections.

Aéroport Le Bourget, Le Bourget

 01-49-92-70-62;
www.museeairespace.fr

 €7 ages 18 and up;
€2 planetarium;
some attractions extra

 Apr–Sept, T–Su 10–6; Oct–Mar,
T–Su 10–5; planetarium W and Sa–Su

 6 and up

the Spitfire and Mustang. A new exhibit devoted to Antoine de Saint-Exupéry honors the pilot who wrote *Le Petit Prince*.

The Grande Galerie includes aviation instruments and equipment from the earliest days of flying machines, along with a superb collection of early aircraft (1879–1918). You can see the passenger section of the 1884 *La France* dirigible, a 1906 Vuia plane, and Henri Fabre's 1910 Hydroplane. Looking at these tiny, fragile constructions makes you appreciate the courage of early aviators. Outside on the runway, you can check out combat planes, rocket launchers, two Ariane rockets, a Boeing 747, and a Concorde. The 3-D film shown in a little movie theater next to the Ariane rockets is usually a hit with kids.

The museum's gift shop has models of aircrafts for kids to build, and the museum's planetarium gives you a close-up view of what astronauts have to face.

EATS FOR KIDS
Good restaurants are few and far between in this area. You can try the museum's **in-house cafeteria**, or bring a picnic and have lunch with the Concorde out on the tarmac. Otherwise, plan your trip between mealtimes.

KEEP IN MIND Your kids, particularly the younger ones, may soon tire of viewing plane after plane in vast hangars and exhibition spaces, especially since there's a lot of walking involved. If you think that might be a problem, limit your visit to the top kid-pleasers: the Grande Galerie, where the rarest and earliest aircraft are displayed, and the Hall Concorde, where kids can get inside a Concorde jet. In mid-June in odd-numbered years, Le Bourget airport hosts the huge Paris air show (official name: Salon Internationale de l'Aéronautique et de l'Espace).

MUSÉE DE L'ORANGERIE

L'Orangerie, set in a corner of the Tuileries gardens, is one of Paris's most appealing small museums. It reopened in 2006 after years of renovation. Built in 1852 as a high-class greenhouse for orange trees, the Orangerie today is a light-filled oasis complete with weeping willows and lily ponds—specifically, Claude Monet's *Nymphéas* (Water Lilies) paintings of them—right in the heart of the city.

Two huge oval rooms—designed especially to display these paintings after Monet decided to offer them to France—offer 360-degree views of the images that Monet was obsessed with late in his life: the play of light on the water-lily-filled ponds in his garden. Each room holds four huge paintings by the master, all curving around the walls to Monet's exacting specifications. One depicts a misty sunrise in lavenders and pale blues, another gleams with the golds and yellows of a sunset over water, others show shimmering flowers, water, and leaves in subtle shades. Natural light floods in through the Orangerie's glass roof, newly restored to exactly what Monet intended (a conventional ceiling added in the 1960s

KEEP IN MIND After a museum visit, younger kids will probably be ready for some running around, and the Tuileries (see Jardin des Tuileries, #41) is an ideal place for that. You can also combine your trip to l'Orangerie with a stroll through the nearby Jardins du Palais-Royal (#39).

MAKE THE MOST OF YOUR TIME Visiting the Orangerie is also a good way to introduce kids to Impressionism, a movement whose name is said to have been inadvertently coined by Louis Leroy, an unsympathetic critic who was mocking the title of Monet's painting *Impression, soleil levant* (now on display in Paris's Musée Marmottan Monet). This lovely little museum has an outstanding collection of Impressionist art by Monet and others (2 rue Louis-Boilly, 16e, métro Passy or La Muette, tel. 01–44–96–50–33, www.marmottan.com).

Jardin des Tuileries near the pl. de
la Concorde, 1er. Métro: Concorde

 €6.50 ages 18 and over

 W–M 9–6

01–44–77–80–07;
www.musee-orangerie.fr

6 and up

was removed during the recent restoration). Stand in the middle of a room and you'll feel surrounded by movement, color, and light.

The museum also displays a small collection of important works by Renoir, Cézanne, Picasso, Rousseau, Matisse, Soutine, Durain, Modigliani, and others. Kids will probably be drawn to Soutine's expressive choirboy; Durain's brightly colored harlequins and musicians; and to the strange little gray dog in a painting by Rousseau of a family on an afternoon outing. Monet and his water lilies are the real stars here, though, and kids usually enjoy the sensation of being surrounded by them.

EATS FOR KIDS La Ferme (55-57 rue St-Roch, tel. 01–40–20–12–12) brings a touch of the French countryside to downtown Paris. This inexpensive self-service eatery specializes in wholesome products from farms just outside the city. Take a basket and choose from the tasty sandwiches, salads, desserts, and fruit juices on hand, then pick a table at the back of the room or picnic on a park bench in the Tuileries or Palais-Royal. For food see also Musée du Louvre (#26), Jardin des Tuileries (#41), and Jardins du Palais-Royal (#39).

MUSÉE DES ARTS ET MÉTIERS

The Musée des Arts et Métiers (Arts and Crafts Museum) would be better called the Museum of Inventions—it doesn't showcase arts and crafts at all, but rather all sorts of technical innovations made from the 16th century to the present. It's a place of inspiration for the world's next Leonardo da Vincis, and those who nurture and admire them.

The museum occupies a spectacular building: the medieval abbey of St-Martin-des-Champs, completely renovated for the 21st century. Containing more than 80,000 objects and documents, it illustrates groundbreaking, world-changing discoveries in the fields of physics, optics, mechanics, telecommunications, and more. Among these testaments to human creativity are everything from weird 18th-century versions of robots to the first movie cameras, invented by brothers Auguste-Marie and Louis-Jean Lumière in the late 19th century. Computer-loving kids should enjoy seeing a *very* early computer, a *machine à calculer* (calculator) invented by Blaise Pascal in 1642. One of the museum's prize objects is a little

60 rue Réaumur, 3e.
Métro: Arts-et-Métiers

01–53–01–82–63;
www.arts-et-metiers.net

 €6.50 ages 25 and up

 T–W and F–Su 10–6, Th 10–9:30

7 and up

24-horsepower monoplane built by the French inventor and flyer Louis Blériot. He used it to become the first person to fly over the English Channel, in 1909.

An exhibit that will probably interest American kids is the one on French sculptor Frédéric-Auguste Bartholdi's designs for the Statue of Liberty. Kids interested in space travel can get a look at the motor used in one of France's Ariane rockets, and a sure kid favorite is the display of quirky automated figures in the museum's Théâtre des Automates. The museum's most stunning object, though, is without a doubt the two-story pendulum created by the French physicist Jean-Bernard-Léon Foucault (1819–1868). Among his many inventions, Foucault used a pendulum to demonstrate that the earth rotates once a day. As Foucault's huge pendulum swings silently back and forth in a vast room, seemingly operated by unseen giants, it gives kids graphic proof that we really are swirling around in space.

KEEP IN MIND

The museum's Théâtre des Automates houses rare automated objects from the 18th, 19th, and 20th centuries. Three times each month, museum staff members put these devices through their paces. Demonstrations are in French but English audio guides are available. Check on the Web site for times and to make reservations.

MAKE THE MOST OF YOUR TIME

Taped guided tours (available in English) help you make sense of the collections (€5). Staff members offer free, kid-friendly demonstrations throughout the museum, daily; ask at the entrance desk for times on the day you visit. The museum also has popular classes for kids 4–13 (€6.50) on Wednesdays, and classes for families on Sundays (€6.50 adults, €4.50 kids 7–13). Both are in French and require advance reservations; you get to build something and take it home. This vast museum contains too much to see in just one visit; the sections on transport and communications are the top kid-pleasers.

MUSÉE D'ORSAY

The vast Musée d'Orsay, a turn-of-the-20th-century railway station imaginatively redesigned by architect Gae Aulenti, still bears marks of its past life, such as the great clock on the Seine-facing facade. (Inside the museum, kids like checking out the clock's workings from the back.) The museum showcases works created from 1848 to 1914, when Paris was recognized as the world's arts capital. Parents may come for the Impressionist paintings, but kids like the variety of objects—from tiny, very early photographs of Paris to gigantic sculptures—presented in a high-ceilinged space with lots of elbow room.

The Musée d'Orsay deserves kudos for making its collection remarkably family-friendly. Pick up a free art-quiz pamphlet, Carnets Parcours Familles (Tours for Families, available in English), when you enter the museum, and you can organize your own museum visit in the form of a game. The museum also gives special 90-minute guided tours for kids ages 5–10 and their families, and other tours just for kids, in which guides bring the collection to life through stories, games, and other activities. These are usually in French, but some guides

KEEP IN MIND Younger kids are typically fans of the big polar bear statue on the upper-level Terrace de Lille, the model of the Opéra de Paris–Garnier (#17), and the charming Art Nouveau and Arts-and-Crafts furniture and decorative objects displayed on the Seine side of the museum.

MAKE THE MOST OF YOUR TIME The museum's excellent two-hour *ateliers des enfants* (classes for kids, €6) are offered in English and include a 45-minute guided tour of the museum followed by a workshop in which children learn about different artistic techniques through hands-on creative activities. The goal is to help them understand what the museum calls "the language of forms." Guided tours for teenagers (often led by a young artist) are offered during French school holidays. For either activity, check times and reserve a spot in advance by calling 01–40–49–47–50. Workshops are for kids only, so parents can take advantage of some adult time!

1 rue de la Légion d'Honneur, 7e.
Métro: Assemblée Nationale

 €8 adults 25 and up

 01-40-49-48-14;
www.musee-orsay.fr

T–W and F 10–6, Th 10–9:45,
Sa–Su 9–6

6 and up

can translate into English. Family-oriented films, theater, and other special events are also organized regularly.

In addition to lush Rodin sculptures, early movie posters, decorative art, and rare examples of early photography, the Musée d'Orsay displays works by some of the world's greatest painters (Delacroix, Ingres, Van Gogh, and others). Favorites among many visitors are works by Impressionists and post-Impressionists, most of which are grouped on the museum's upper level. Along with paintings by Monet, Manet, Cézanne, Sisley, Pissarro, and Renoir, is Dégas's sculpture *Petite danseuse de quatorze ans* (Little 14-Year-Old Dancer), a model for budding ballerinas. The Moreau–Nélaton room on the ground floor displays two of France's most famous paintings, Manet's *Déjeuner sur l'herbe* (kids can look for the little frog at the picnic) and Monet's *Coquelicots*, with its vivid red poppies.

EATS FOR KIDS The museum's **Café du Lion** under the giant clock serves snacks, light dishes, and afternoon tea. It can get extremely crowded during lunch and dinner. An elegant (and more expensive) alternative is the **Restaurant du Musée d'Orsay** on the museum's first floor. On Tuesday and Sunday mornings, an **organic food market** on the boulevard Raspail (métro: Sèvres-Babylone) has great picnic treats. For park benches, try the little square des Missions Étrangères off the rue du Bac or the square Boucicaut near the Sèvres-Babylone métro; both have kids' play areas.

MUSÉE DU LOUVRE

Just because the world's most famous museum is filled with priceless treasures like Leonardo da Vinci's *Mona Lisa* and the *Venus de Milo* doesn't mean that kids will like it. The sheer size of this former palace makes it overwhelming for everyone, children especially. But that doesn't mean you should avoid it. Your best strategy is to think of the Louvre as a long-term project, and plan to see only a small part of it each time you come. Pick up a free map at the museum's entrance and narrow your visit down to a few key areas. "Objective Louvre" brochures (available in English) lead you on thematic tours of the collections; you might concentrate on the art of eating, for example.

The basic organization of the Louvre is actually quite simple, with three main wings—Richelieu, Sully, and Denon. Of the three, Sully is probably your best bet with youngsters, because it's the wing with the mummies and other artifacts from ancient Egypt, including the realistic statue known as the *Seated Scribe*. You can see sarcophagi, papyrus, and mummies of all sorts—people, cats, even fish—all wrapped up in their creepy bandages. You'll also find

MAKE THE MOST OF YOUR TIME The least-crowded times to visit the Louvre are Wednesday and Friday evenings. The Rue de Rivoli entrance usually has the shortest lines, at any time; to avoid long lines entirely, use your Paris Museum Pass (see Get Ready, Get Set) or buy your tickets in advance on the museum's Web site or at various Paris locations. The underground Carrousel du Louvre shopping mall adjoining the Louvre is a good source for souvenirs and gifts. The Nature et Découvertes store in the mall (tel. 01–47–03–47–43, www.natureetdecouvertes.fr) organizes free crafts workshops for kids, and family-friendly nature-oriented tours in and around Paris.

34–36 quai du Louvre and 99 rue de Rivoli, 1er. Métro: Louvre

01-44-11-33-99; www.louvre.fr

€9.50 adults 18 and up, €6 W and F, 6–9:45, free 1st Su of month; temporary exhibits extra

M, Th, and Sa–Su, 9–6, W and F, 9–9:45

7 and up

intricate Roman mosaics and Etruscan art, along with the Greek masterpieces the *Venus de Milo* and the *Winged Victory of Samothrace*.

The Denon Wing has paintings from the Italian Renaissance, and that means the *Mona Lisa*, which is sealed up under glass and always surrounded by worshippers. Unless you show up first thing in the morning, you'll have to nudge your way through crowds to get a prolonged glimpse. The Denon Wing also includes the grandiose Galerie d'Apollon, which has a potential kid-pleaser, King Louis XV's jewel-encrusted crown. In the Richelieu wing, kids will probably be impressed by the re-creation of the sumptuous palace of King Sargon II of Assyria. Outside the Louvre, the I.M. Pei pyramid over the museum's main entrance is surrounded by fountains and a wide paved area where kids can run around. It's especially spectacular at night when the Louvre's exterior walls are dramatically lit.

EATS FOR KIDS
Within the museum you'll find two **restaurants** and **five snack bars**, including quiet **Café Denon** (for light meals), and **Café Richelieu**, whose terrace overlooks the I.M. Pei pyramid. **Universal Resto** (tel. 01–47–03–96–58) is a self-service food court in the Carrousel du Louvre shopping mall.

KEEP IN MIND The Louvre organizes excellent workshops for kids 4–12; call 01–40–20–51–77 for subjects and times. Around 30 different workshops are offered. In a recent one, kids located portraits of Cupid in the collections and then played games and tried on costumes to figure out which portraits they preferred. Guided tours are also organized for kids 6–8 or 8–12 (€3.50), and special guided tours and workshops for the whole family can be arranged (tel. 01–40–20–50–50). These activities are in French but most staff members speak English. Reserve at least two weeks in advance for any activity.

A prominent feature of this museum's unconventional design, by architect Jean Nouvel, is a set of colorful boxes on stilts, above a garden overlooking the Seine. It decidedly doesn't fit into its surroundings, but then neither did the Tour Eiffel when it was built.

From the glass-walled entrance with its 46-foot-tall totem pole, you walk up a spiraling ramp around a transparent tower filled with musical instruments, which takes you to a vast space where you wander around viewing the 3,500 or so objects in the museum's main collection (the museum has 300,000 works of art and artifacts in total from Oceania, Asia, the Middle East, Africa, and the Americas).

Kids will like the nonlinear organization, dim lighting (to protect light-sensitive objects), and low walls that look like they're made from mud. The museum employs innovative multimedia techniques—drumbeats rumbling in the background near an exhibit of African drums, or a video of people hunting in tall grass shown next to a set of weapons from

EATS FOR KIDS The museum has two restaurants: the elegant **Les Ombres**, with cuisines from all over the world and views of the Tour Eiffel (reservations required, 01–47–53–68–00), and the more affordable **Café Branly** overlooking the garden, which has special kids' menus at lunch and for afternoon tea. For food see also Tour Eiffel (#1).

MAKE THE MOST OF YOUR TIME The museum offers various classes (in French) for kids 6–12, including story hours for younger kids, classes to teach kids what an anthropologist does, and sessions that permits children to donate toys and make their own out of recycled materials. Films and special shows for kids (and others for teenagers and adults) are also organized regularly. Classes are offered on Wednesdays and Saturdays, reservations necessary (tel. 01–56–61–71–72).

37 Quai Branly, 7e.
Métro: Alma-Marceau or Bir-Hakeim

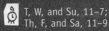
€8.50 ages 18 and over,
special exhibits extra

T, W, and Su, 11–7;
Th, F, and Sa, 11–9

01–56–61–70–00;
www.quaibranly.fr

6 and over

the Solomon Islands—to help you understand what these objects actually meant and were used for in the cultures that produced them.

Interspersed with ceremonial robes and statues you'll find video screens showing films on dance (that often inspire kids to dance along), tattooing, and initiation rituals. Another high point are gorgeous masks that your kids will learn are not Halloween costumes, but rather symbols whose meanings children in other cultures understood. Some of the masks are adorned with shells and even spiderwebs.

This relative newcomer to the Paris museum scene has its critics (some loathe the design, others insist its collections should be returned to the cultures that produced them). However, most come away impressed by the museum's variety, beauty, and energy.

KEEP IN MIND Audio tours (available in English, €5 per person or €7 for two adults) and the Parcours en Famille tour for families (in French, €2.50 per person) help you make sense of the collections. There's also audio (in French) for the River section of the main collection, which focuses on different cultures' concepts of space. If you get lost while visiting the main collection, look down; the floors are color-coded (blue for the Americas, for example). Audio tours in English are also available for the museum's innovative temporary exhibits.

MUSÉE EN HERBE

I f your kids say they hate museums, bring them here and prove them wrong. Paris's first museum just for children (*en herbe* means "young sprouts," as in kids) believes that the best way for youngsters to learn is to have fun and move around. Almost everything on display is meant to be touched, fiddled with, or laughed at, and children don't just walk through exhibits; they're given a treasure map that guides them on a quest. While small kids manipulate geometric objects in kid-friendly colors and sizes, bigger kids can create art on their own faces using the makeup that's always on hand.

Most permanent exhibits have to do with the arts—interactive displays illustrating perspective or color combinations, for example—but the innovative temporary exhibits (changing every six months or so) broaden the focus. Every exhibit is fun for kids. One recent exhibit, *Quel Artiste ce Matisse!* (That Matisse, What an Artist!) lets kids help Matisse find his glasses, open the window in Matisse's painting *Fenêtre au rideau egyptien* (Window with Egyptian Curtain), and try to draw (as Matisse did when he was ill) with a

MAKE THE MOST OF YOUR TIME Everything in this museum is in French, including the workshops, but many staff members speak English and everything is so hands-on that kids should be able to follow what's going on. Workshops for kids 5–12 are held on Wednesdays, Saturdays, Sundays, and holidays at 3:30 and 5, and daily during long school vacations. Workshops for kids 2½ to 4½ are held on Wednesdays and during school holidays at 11 and 2.

21 rue Hérold, 1e.
Métro: Etienne Marcel

01–40–67–97–66;
www.musee-en-herbe.com

 €4; workshops €8

daily 10–6

3–12

pencil stuck on the end of a fishing pole. The Boîtes à Couleurs de Picasso (Picasso's Coloring Box) exhibit let kids dress up like one of Picasso's harlequins or try to re-create *Les Demoiselles d'Avignon*, among other fun exercises, while the Suivez Le Gout (Follow That Taste) exhibit—organized with the help of a wine museum in the Loire Valley—let kids test their ability to recognize different tastes.

Along with the exhibits, the museum organizes special classes for kids of all ages in which they can do all sorts of things, from painting pictures and creating sculpture to putting together machines or putting on a show. Kids visit the special exhibit and then work in groups to create something based on what they've just seen. There's even a special baby *atelier* (workshop) for kids 2½–4½. This place is museum as playtime, and it's been entertaining kids and teaching them things since 1975.

KEEP IN MIND
Guided tours for the whole family are given Monday, Wednesday, Saturday, and Sunday at 10:30 and 1. Wednesdays and weekends are the best days to come here, because on other days the museum usually hosts groups from local schools. Reserve well in advance for workshops and tours.

EATS FOR KIDS II **Tre** (3 rue des Petits-Carreaux, tel. 01–40–13–03–29), an upscale pizza joint with bright red decor, is a good choice for lunch or dinner. Or, if you feel like a short stroll, do what the Parisians do—grab a picnic lunch and head over to the tiny Square du Vert Galant, at the very tip of the Ile de la Cité, just off the Pont Neuf. From this vantage point you're right in the heart of Paris, with great views of the Pont des Arts and many major monuments, including the Tour Eiffel, Grand Palais, and the Académie Française. See also Jardin des Halles [#43], the Jardin du Palais-Royal [#39], or the Jardin des Tuileries [#41].

MUSÉE GRÉVIN

Want to see Spiderman stand absolutely still? You can at this museum, because he's made out of wax, and so are a lot of other people you may or may not recognize. There's something slightly creepy about wax museums, with their eerily lifelike figures frozen in place as though under a magic spell, but everyone usually has fun picking out people they know. And this wax museum, created in 1882, has the added bonus of providing a very vivid tour through history.

In the section on French history, you'll see King François I meeting England's King Henry VIII in 1520, Louis XIV at a sumptuous party at the Château de Versailles, Marie-Antoinette in her cell in the Concièrgerie prison, Napoléon drinking tea with Josephine, and the French revolutionary leader Jean-Paul Marat murdered in his bathtub. (By the way, the bathtub here really is the one Marat died in; this is one tableau that's not for little kids.) Other sections focus on movie stars and on movers and shakers past and present, who are displayed in elaborately decorated tableaux complete with background sounds.

KEEP IN MIND The nearby passage Jouffroy, one of Paris's picturesque covered shopping streets, has two stores that specialize in toys, dolls, and furnishings for doll houses: Pain d'Épices (29 pass. Jouffroy, tel. 01–47–70–08–68) and La Boîte à Joujoux (41 pass. Jouffroy, tel. 01–48–24–58–37).

EATS FOR KIDS Homesick? Bite the bullet and head to the **Hard Rock Cafe** (14 bd. Montmartre, tel. 01–53–24–60–00) to chow down on burgers, fajitas, and other American-style treats. Jugglers, singers, and who knows what else may be on hand to entertain you. For old-fashioned French fare, try the atmospheric **Chartier** (7 rue Faubourg-Montmartre, tel. 01–47–70–86–29), one of the oldest bistros in Paris, where you can sample inexpensive *pâté*, *crudités* (raw vegetables in vinaigrette), and roast chicken with *frites* (fries). **Le Valentin** (30 pass. Jouffroy, tel. 01–47–70–88–50) is a cozy tearoom that also serves lunch.

10 bd. Montmartre, 9e.
Métro: Richelieu-Drouot

 01-47-70-85-05;
www.grevin.com

 €20 ages 15 and up,
€12 children 6-14;
guided tours extra

 M-F 10-6:30, Sa-Su and during
school holidays 9-7

 7 and up

As for the contemporary personalities, fame is fleeting and so are these figures. They come and go depending on whether the people they represent are in the news; it's a formula that's attracted more than 45 million visitors to the museum since it opened. Kids are bound to spot some familiar faces, from Lara Croft: Tomb Raider to basketball star Tony Parker, George W. Bush, and French mime artist Marcel Marceau.

Kids usually like having their pictures taken while standing next to their favorite celebrities. Another hit is the Palais des Mirages, a sound-and-light extravaganza created for the 1900 world's fair that's still wowing audiences. The Snapshots of the 20th Century exhibit has 10 tableaux that recreate great moments of the past century, including Neil Armstrong's first step on the moon and the fall of the Berlin wall. All the tableaux blur the thin line between illusion and reality—which is what this museum is all about.

MAKE THE MOST OF YOUR TIME The museum's
Parcours Découverte (discovery tour), geared to kids 7-12 but open to adults, lets kids touch some wax figures and learn about how they're made. For example, they learn that the figures have real human hair, around 500,000 hairs per figure, and that each hair has to be attached to the wax separately. Who knew? There's also a guided visit just for kids 7-12 (in French) that lets kids dress up as princesses or pages before the tour.

MUSÉE NATIONAL DU MOYEN ÂGE

Travel with your kids back to the Middle Ages and have a close encounter with a mythical beast at this kid-friendly Left Bank museum. In a medieval mansion that once belonged to the Cluny abbots, the National Museum of the Middle Ages contains a rich collection of art and artifacts, but its most famous treasure is *La dame à la licorne* (The Lady and the Unicorn), a series of six 15th-century tapestries that depict strange beasts and a mysterious lady.

Kids have fun trying to work out the complex symbolism of the tapestries, five of which represent the five senses; the sixth, titled *À mon seul désir* (To My Only Desire), has provoked debate for centuries. Even younger kids should enjoy the six tapestries' exotic plants and animals, particularly the adorable unicorn, who, in the *La vue* (Sight) tapestry, smiles at itself in a mirror while its front feet rest on the lady's lap. Other items in the collection that should appeal to kids are medieval weapons and armor, a model of the Gallo-Roman baths next to the museum, and a number of objects that evoke daily life in the Middle Ages, such as a child's sandal from the 14th or 15th century.

EATS FOR KIDS Fish (69 rue de Seine, tel. 01–43–54–34–69) will please seafood-lovers, and this restaurant's gourmet delights range beyond seafood. The friendly American owner is also the proprietor of the excellent La Dernière Goutte wine shop nearby. **The Tea Caddy** (14 rue St-Julien-Le-Pauvre, tel. 01–43–54–15–56) is a cozy restaurant-tearoom that serves scrambled eggs, pastries, and other good things. **Café Maure de la Mosquée de Paris** (39 rue Geoffroy-St-Hilaire, tel. 01–43–31–18–14), adjoining Paris's mosque, is a good choice for mint tea and pastries. For food see also Cathédrale de Notre-Dame-de-Paris (#60) and Jardin du Luxembourg (#40).

6 pl. Paul-Painlevé, 5e. Métro: Cluny

 Sept–May, €8 adults
26 and up, €6 ages
18–25

 M and W–Su 9:15–5:45

01-53-73-78-00; www.musee-moyenage.fr;
www.culture.gouv.fr

7 and up, garden all ages

Outside the museum, along the boulevard St-Michel, you can check out the vestiges of the Gallo-Roman baths on which the museum stands; they date from the time of Marcus Aurelius: the 2nd century AD. Youngsters will prefer the museum's public garden along boulevard St-Germain, where vegetables and flowers typical of gardens in the Middle Ages have been planted in fanciful patterns. There's a play area with climbing equipment for younger kids, while older kids might want to explore the garden's medicinal simples section, with the nine key plants used in medieval medicine.

You can visit the garden without touring the museum. It has several benches, great for resting tired feet in a peaceful setting while you check out walls that date from the 1st to the 15th centuries. And it's all right here in the heart of Paris.

KEEP IN MIND In the Middle Ages, people believed that the unicorn's horn could magically detect poisons and purify water. The unicorn was said to have the body of a horse, the beard and feet of a goat, a flowing tail, and a spiraling horn all its own.

MAKE THE MOST OF YOUR TIME
Ask for the free Comme des Images (Like Pictures) brochure for kids when you enter the museum; even if your kids don't read French, it will help them get a handle on the imagery they will find here. The museum's excellent one-hour guided tours for families (with kids 7–12) focus on helping you understand life in the Middle Ages. In the crafts classes (in French, €10) kids might learn techniques of medieval manuscript decoration, architecture, garden design, or metalworking. Tours and classes are offered on two Wednesdays per month and during some school holidays (tel. 01–53–73–78–16 for reservations).

MUSÉE PICASSO

Note: This museum is closed for renovation until Sept 2012; this review reflects the status of the museum before the renovations, so confirm details before you go. Devoted to the 20th-century's most famous artist, the Musée Picasso fills a palatial 17th-century mansion in the heart of the Marais district. A real effort has been made to get kids enthusiastic about the art displayed here through guided art-appreciation tours and films and classes (in French). During the tours, given on Wednesdays and Sundays, kids take a good look at an artwork, ask questions about it, and discuss it with a very competent staff member (parents are allowed to tag along on the Sunday tours). Even if your children can't participate in these activities, they should enjoy the art in the collection. Among the thousands of works by Picasso are 200 paintings, sculptures, and ceramics and more than 3,000 drawings and prints. The museum also displays Picasso's personal art collection, which includes works by Derain, Cézanne, Modigliani, Renoir, Rousseau, Braque, and other 20th-century greats whom he admired.

KEEP IN MIND Pablo Picasso (1881–1973) was born in Málaga, Spain, where his great artistic talent was recognized very early; the first public showing of his works was held when he was just 16. After a visit to Paris three years later, he moved to France and stayed.

MAKE THE MOST OF YOUR TIME Take refuge in one of Paris's newest public parks, the peaceful little Jardin Francs-Bourgeois-Rosiers, which you enter at 35 rue des Francs-Bourgeois. It has park benches, a kids' play area, and a patch of lawn for toddlers, and it's surrounded by beautiful 17th-century buildings. If seeing Picasso's works inspires your kids to get creative, visit Rougier et Pié (13 bd. des Filles-de-Calvaire, tel. 01–44–54–81–00), where you'll find all kinds of art supplies as well as high-quality craft materials. Staff members regularly demonstrate techniques.

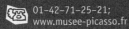 Hôtel Salé, 5 rue de Thorigny, 3e.
Métro: Chemin Vert, Saint-Paul

 €7.70 adults 26 and up,
€5.70 adults 18–25

01–42–71–25–21;
www.musee-picasso.fr

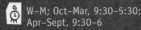 W–M; Oct–Mar, 9:30–5:30;
Apr–Sept, 9:30–6

 10 and up

Children often seem to respond better to contemporary art than adults do. They accept it on its own terms, and, in the case of Picasso, respond to his playfulness. Kids of all ages wander through the galleries here, picking out works they like. Some prefer the "pink period," others the "blue period," but most are impressed by the huge *Têtes monumentales* (Monumental Heads) in the sculpture gallery. After viewing the collection, take a break in the museum's lovely garden or pick out an art poster in the gift shop.

In case your children ask, the building's name, Hôtel Salé, means "salted town house," which came from the fact that its original owner, Aubert de Fontenay, made his fortune by being the sole collector of a French tax on salt. There's a certain poetic justice in this, because after Picasso's death his heirs gave his private collection to the French government in lieu of paying inheritance taxes, and the government in turn created this museum to house the collection. Any way you look at it, it's a museum that taxes built.

EATS FOR KIDS The museum's in-house **cafeteria** overlooking the garden offers quiches, soup, salads, and afternoon tea. **Brocco** (180 rue du Temple, tel. 01–42–72–19–81) is a pastry shop and tearoom with gooey pastries and an elaborately painted 1889 ceiling. **Le Loir dans la Théière** (3 rue des Rosiers, tel. 01–42–72–90–61), a cozy tearoom, serves pastries and light lunches. For food see also Centre National d'Art et de Culture Georges Pompidou (#59), Musée de la Magie et des Automates (#32), Musée d'Art et d'Histoire du Judaïsme (#33), and Place des Vosges and the Marais (#6).

MUSÉE RODIN

The elegant 18th-century Hôtel Biron, Rodin's home for the last decade of his life, contains many of the sculptor's best-known works, including *Les Bourgeois de Calais* (The Burghers of Calais) and *Le Penseur* (The Thinker). Many of the sculptures are displayed in the 5-plus-acre garden surrounding the house, which has beautifully planted flower beds, trees, a sandbox, and lots of benches. You'll usually find Parisian parents reading quietly here while their babies doze and their older kids run around and play. Rodin's massive yet fluid and lifelike sculptures are a calm background in this peaceful scene.

If you thought of Rodin as a struggling artist working in a tiny garret, think again; his mansion is an elegant white stone building with tall windows overlooking the garden. Within, you find some of Rodin's smaller sculptures as well as drawings and art from his personal collection—including works by Monet, Van Gogh, Camille Claudel, and other artists Rodin knew—all displayed in the mansion's large, high-ceilinged rooms.

EATS FOR KIDS The Rodin Museum's reasonably priced cafeteria and tearoom, **Le Jardin de Varenne** (tel. 01–45–55–84–39), offers many choices of sandwiches, salads, and desserts, but the main draw is the location overlooking the museum's lovely garden. It's one of the most peaceful places to have lunch in this busy neighborhood. Tiny, budget-priced **Chez Germaine** (30 rue Pierre-Leroux, tel. 01–42–73–28–34) serves classic bistro dishes like leeks in vinaigrette and *poulet au riz* (stewed chicken with rice). For food see also Tour Eiffel (#1) and Hôtel National des Invalides (#46).

77 rue de Varenne, 7e.
Métro: Varenne

 01-44-18-61-10;
www.musee-rodin.fr

 Museum (permanent and temporary exhibits) and garden €10 adults 25 and up; €5 18–25; garden only €1 adults 18 and up; kids' tour and class €6

Museum and garden T–Su, 10–5:45

All ages

Although younger kids usually prefer the museum's garden (where they can run around) to its interior (where they need to be sedate and well behaved), older kids enjoy seeing the varied works of art and maybe even trying a little sculpting themselves. Every Wednesday afternoon from 2:30 to 4, and several times a week during school holidays, the museum organizes combined tours and art classes for kids: one session for children 6–8, another for youths 9–12. (While your kids are busy in their classes, you can take a tour of the museum's collection yourself.) Following a guided tour of the collection (in French), children are encouraged to have a close encounter with one of the museum's artworks and then to try their hands at drawing or sculpting in wax, clay, or plaster, expressing a particular theme. They can even take their finished piece with them. Though sessions are in French, even non-French-speakers should be able to enjoy these popular hands-on lessons, which bring kids in close touch with one of France's best-known artists.

MAKE THE MOST OF YOUR TIME

This small museum is definitely committed to helping kids perceive art in new ways. Check the Web site for activities on offer during your stay in Paris and reserve well in advance for the very popular kids' tours and workshops (tel. 01–44–18–61–24).

KEEP IN MIND In his day, Rodin's realistic style was very new and, at the beginning of his career, much criticized. Examples of his devotion to realism include *L'Homme au nez cassé* (The Man with the Broken Nose). Rodin's model was a local handyman named Bibi, whom Rodin depicted realistically, broken nose and all, while still employing elements of classic Greek sculpture (the hair and blank eyes). Rodin continued to draw inspiration from this rugged face for other works. Kids should take a close look at the *La Porte d'Enfer* and *Les Bourgeois de Calais* to see if they can find someone who looks like Bibi.

MUSÉE VIVANT DU CHEVAL

Once upon a time (in 1719), a French prince, Louis-Henri de Bourbon, prince de Condé, had a vision: when he died, he would be reborn—as a horse. The prince, who was very rich, decided to build a horse château worthy of a princely stallion. He asked the most famous architect of the time to create Les Grandes Écuries (The Great Stables) facing his own fabulous Château de Chantilly, in the middle of a huge forest north of Paris. The prince died, perhaps becoming one of the 300 or so horses that lived in Les Grandes Écuries throughout the 18th century. Here they were visited by the likes of King Louis XV.

Today, Les Grandes Écuries is still the home of pampered horses, as well as of the Musée Vivant du Cheval (Living Museum of the Horse), which welcomes around 200,000 visitors a year. Kids like seeing the stable complex, where around 30 well-groomed horses swish their tails in their luxurious boxes in a huge hall with a vaulted stone ceiling. All sorts of objects relating to horses over the ages fill the museum's more than 30 exhibit rooms.

EATS FOR KIDS For lunch or afternoon tea, try **Aux Goûters Champêtres** (tel. 03–44–57–46–21), with an outdoor terrace, and the more formal **La Capitainerie du Château** (tel. 03–44–57–15–89), which serves a lavish buffet brunch on weekends (reservations necessary). Both are inside the château.

MAKE THE MOST OF YOUR TIME Several trains per day run from the Gare du Nord to Chantilly–Les Gouvieux (30 minutes), but you will have about a 20-minute walk from the train station in Chantilly to the museum (or take a taxi, though lines can be long). By car from Paris, take the A1 highway from the Porte de la Chapelle, on the northern edge of Paris, and head north to the Survilliers-Chantilly exit. Signs in the center of Chantilly point you to the Musée Vivant du Cheval. Chantilly's tourist office (60 av. Maréchal-Joffre, tel. 03–44–67–37–37) has information in English and rents bikes.

Les Grandes Écuries, Château de Chantilly, Chantilly

03-44-57-40-40, www.museevivantducheval.fr; château 03-44-62-62-62, www.chateaudechantilly.com

Museum €19 adults 18 and up, €8 children 4–17; combined ticket château, museum, and park €19 adults, €8 children; shows extra; château and park €10 adults, €8 children 4–17

Apr–Oct, M and W–Su 10–6; Nov–Mar, M and W–Su 10:30–5:30; château hrs vary

3 and up

The main attractions, however, are the equestrian shows performed regularly in the museum's elegant *manège* (ring). You sit very near the beautiful horses, who, along with their riders, wear elaborate costumes, while an orchestra plays in the background. Every year in December, special Christmas shows for kids are given, in which Santa (riding a horse or donkey) has trouble delivering his gifts. He's helped by various characters, all of whom perform spectacular acts on horseback.

The Château de Chantilly (guided visits only) contains the Musée Condé, which has an art collection considered one of the best in France, but neither attraction is geared to kids. Children are sure to like the elegant park, however, parts of which were designed by the great Le Nôtre, who also designed the gardens at Versaille. As parents admire fountains and flowers, kids can run along the graveled paths or get lost in a new labyrinth. There's also a little train that's a boon for tired toddlers.

KEEP IN MIND Equestrian shows take place on Sunday and include a very popular show for kids at Christmas (shows €21 ages 18 and up, €16 ages 4–18; includes museum admission; tel. 03–44–57–40–40 for reservations, or buy advance tickets online). While you're in Chantilly, sample the local specialty, *crème Chantilly* (whipped cream), sold atop cookies at stands around town.

MUSÉUM NATIONAL D'HISTOIRE NATURELLE

France's natural-history museum is actually several museums in the Jardin des Plantes, each focusing on a different aspect of natural history. The showcase collection is the state-of-the-art Grande Galerie de l'Évolution (Grand Gallery of Evolution) with its stunning parade of life-size models of African animals—giraffes, elephants, zebras, and much, much more—in the main hall. The Grande Galerie clearly illustrates the concept of biodiversity in ways children can understand, and focuses on the need for people to protect the natural world.

Using the latest bells and whistles, such as interactive touch screens and games, this gallery makes natural history exciting and fun. Displays showing animal habitats come with light shows and sounds to bring the habitats alive. A skeleton of a blue whale hangs from the ceiling, too. There is plenty of room to move around the huge, modern, perfectly lit space.

The ground floor of the Grande Galerie is devoted to aquatic and marine life, and you'll see all sorts of sea creatures as well as an exhibit that magnifies grains of sand 800 times and

MAKE THE MOST OF YOUR TIME Also within the museum complex are the Galerie de Minéralogie (Mineralogy Gallery), with a huge collection of gemstones, meteorites, and rocks; and the combined Galeries de Paléontologie et d'Anatomie Comparée (Paleontology and Comparative Anatomy Galleries), which display an impressive collection of animal skeletons, including one of a carnivorous dinosaur that roamed in Utah 150 million years ago. You will also see many pickled creatures that can be scary for younger kids. Admission for either gallery: €6 ages 14 and over (or €4 if you bought a ticket to another attraction in the Jardin des Plantes the same day); €4 ages 4–13.

36 rue Geoffroy-St-Hilaire, 5e.
Métro: Jussieu, Austerlitz

01–40–79–30–00;
www.mnhn.fr

Evolution gallery €7 ages
25 and up; other galleries extra

M and W–Su 10–6

4 and up

may make you never want to have another picnic on the beach. The first floor focuses on biodiversity on land, and one kid favorite is bound to be the enormous elephant, Siam (stuffed), who died in 1997 the same day as his trainer and ended up here (without the trainer). Other exhibits show animals in different habitats. Don't miss the Salle de Découverte (Discovery Room) on this level, where kids can play games, look through microscopes, and use fun gadgets to learn more about nature. You'll have trouble getting your children out of this place.

On the next floor up, you'll find many exhibits on evolution, including ones that focus on humanity's effect on the global environment as the world's population grows. One room here is devoted to extinct animals, including the dodo and the Seychelles tortoise. Kids learn a lot about Mother Nature in this exceptional museum, but they're guaranteed to have fun in the process.

EATS FOR KIDS

Within the Grande Galerie is a **cafeteria** where you have a choice of sandwiches overlooking the parade of animals on the ground floor. Where else can you have lunch with a giraffe? For food see also Jardin des Plantes (#42), Jardin de Sculpture en Plein Air (#44), and Arènes de Lutèce (#66).

KEEP IN MIND The Evolution Gallery regularly organizes special guided tours, workshops, and other activities (in French) for adults and for kids that help bring the collections to life. Check the Web site for details of activities during the time you'll be in Paris and reserve in advance for the workshops. As for the many stuffed real animals on display here, they don't look creepy at all, but rather very realistic in their carefully reconstructed habitats. Note that this museum can get extremely crowded on weekends and on Wednesdays (when many French kids are out of school) from September through June.

OPÉRA DE PARIS–GARNIER

If you want your children to see an architectural landmark that sums up everything that was Paris in the mid-19th century, the Opéra de Paris–Garnier is the place to go. Dripping with gilt and covered with every possible kind of adornment, from charging horses to the heads (sculpted in stone) of composers, the Opéra de Paris–Garnier was considered the height of sophistication in the days when Paris was recognized as the world's cultural capital, and when this was the city's only opera house. Even the most blasé kids can't help but be impressed by all the red plush, gilt, and general overblown elegance of the opera house's interior.

Take a guided tour of the Opéra de Paris–Garnier (tours in English are available), or stroll around on your own to check out the monumental marble staircase, the 11,000-square-meter (118,000-square-foot) stage, and the main auditorium's fanciful ceiling, painted by Marc Chagall in 1964. Whether you choose to tour the Opéra on your own or with a guide, make sure its famous auditorium (the Salle de Spectacle) will be open during your visit;

KEEP IN MIND Check out the enormous crystal chandelier in the Opéra's red-and-gold auditorium. It used to hold hundreds of candles, but now it's electric. You wouldn't want it to fall on your head: it weighs 8 tons. The question is, how did they light all those candles?

EATS FOR KIDS **Fauchon** (30 pl. de la Madeleine, tel. 01–42–65–17–60, www. fauchon.fr) has all kinds of goodies (perhaps even Opéra honey) to take out or eat in. Another famous upscale food shop/restaurant on the square is **Hédiard** at #21 (tel. 01–43–12–88–88). If you're looking for something more down-to-earth and don't mind sitting elbow-to-elbow with Parisians, try the **Foyer de la Madeleine** (tel. 01–47–42–39–84) under Madeleine church (entrance on the church's east side). Volunteers serve a full lunch on weekdays (except in August) for the bargain price of €8 (drink and coffee included) plus a one-time €3 membership fee.

8 rue Scribe, 9e. Métro: Opéra

 08–92–89–90–90;
www.operadeparis.fr

 €9 ages 26 and up, €5 ages
 10–25; guided tours €12 ages
26 and up, €9 ages 10–25,
€6 under 10

Daily 10–5; English tours Wed, Sa–Su
(daily July–Aug) 11:30 and 2:30

 8 and up

it's closed during rehearsals for performances, except during lunchtime (1–2) when performers and musicians take a break. Opera and dance performances are given at the Opéra de Paris–Garnier year-round, but none are geared to kids. For kid-friendly concerts, visit the city's other opera house, the Opéra de Paris—Bastille (see Make the Most of Your Time).

On the 90-minute guided tours (which aren't specifically for kids, but guides are usually happy to answer kids' questions), you and your children will learn all sorts of surprising facts about the Opéra Garnier, including that trout were once raised in a pond beneath the building, and that bees live on the Opéra Garnier's roof and their honey is sold in the high-class Fauchon food shop on the place de la Madeleine. You'll also learn a lot about the Opéra de Paris–Garnier's most famous resident, the Phantom of the Opera.

MAKE THE MOST OF YOUR TIME The Opéra de Paris's Jeune Public series of dance and musical performances geared to kids and the whole family are staged throughout the year (check www.operadeparis.fr for the schedule). These shows feature all kinds of music and dance, from baroque to hip-hop (€16 ages 13 and up, €5 ages 12 and under). All are staged at the Opéra de Paris's other opera house, the state-of-the-art Opéra de Paris–Bastille on the place de la Bastille (120 rue de Lyon, tel. 01–40–01–17–89).

Does your family love to play cards and board games? If so, come to this innovative game-playing center and games store, where you can find great new games that you'd probably never come across otherwise, since most aren't distributed in the United States. Oya has a collection of hundreds of games that you can play there and/or buy to take home. This nonsmoking, no-alcohol establishment is a good spot to take a break on a rainy day, and perhaps to find an out-of-the-ordinary souvenir of your time in Paris.

Start by choosing a table (the center has several tables and can handle up to 60 game-players at a time), and ask the very friendly, English-speaking staff for suggestions of games that will best fit your group's ages and interests. A staff member will then bring you a game to try out and will explain the rules to you in English. Staff members are also ready to help if you have questions while playing. You can play a game as long and as many times as you like. It's a good idea to play a game more than once instead of immediately

MAKE THE MOST OF YOUR TIME
Paris is many cities, and one of the best examples of that is the *quartier chinois* (Chinatown). In an area blighted by characterless high-rises, people from all over Asia—and elsewhere—have created a dynamic, colorful neighborhood. Stroll along the streets around the Parc de Choisy a few blocks south of Oya and you'll see many tempting shops, including Tang Frères (44 av. d'Ivry, tel. 01–45–85–19–85), where you'll find every possible kind of Oriental food item, along with cooking utensils, toys, and takeout treats. Sample them in the park, which has a merry-go-round, a puppet theater, and play areas.

25 rue de la Reine Blanche, 13e.
Métro: Gobelins

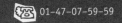
01-47-07-59-59

1st game €5 per person,
€6 with a drink; 2nd game
€3 per person

T–Sa 2–12, Su 2–9

6 and up

trying another one, because this lets you get to know the game better. If you want to try a second game, there's a small extra charge.

Some games the whole family should enjoy are Métro (based on the Paris métro), Pique-Plume, and Take It Easy, but your best bet is to ask the staff to recommend a game that's right for your group. Of course, you're always welcome to buy a game to take home. Oya's shelves are full of all kinds of games at very reasonable prices, from around €9 up to €50. Oya is a great place to meet people, and the staff can set you up with another group of players if you like. Trying to trounce each other in a game is a fun way to make new friends.

KEEP IN MIND

When it comes to asking staff for a game suggestion, be specific. Let the person know the types of games your family likes and how much experience you have in playing them. That way you're more likely to get a game that's right for you.

EATS FOR KIDS Oya sells sodas, tea, coffee, juices, and ice cream. Bakeries and take-out shops are nearby. **Liliana Café** (39 rue Pascal, tel. 01–43–31–00–98) is a modern brasserie where you can sample up-to-date French dishes at a fairly reasonable price. **La Tropicale** (180 bd. Vincent-Auriol, tel. 01–42–16–87–27) offers quiche, pastries, and delicious ice cream (try the strawberry-mint). **Sinorama** (118 av. de Choisy, tel. 01–53–82–09–51) specializes in Asian delicacies like *canard aux fleurs de lotus* (duck with lotus blossoms) and creative vegetarian dishes.

PALAIS DE CHAILLOT

The grandiose Palais de Chaillot, created for the 1937 Paris world's fair, contains two museums kids enjoy: the new Cité de l'Architecture et du Patrimoine (Museum and Research Center on Architecture and Patrimony, or Cité Chaillot) and the Musée de la Marine (Naval History Museum). The third museum here, the Musée de l'Homme, lost most of its collection to the Quai Branly museum (see #25) and is partly closed down.

The Cité Chaillot focuses on France's magnificent heritage of architecture from the 12th to the 21st centuries. Using all the latest high-tech tools, the museum makes a big effort to get kids thinking about how buildings are created, and the kids' workshops here are some of the most innovative on offer in Paris (check the Web site to see what's happening during your visit; prices and hours vary). Kids can use computers to design their dream houses, practice medieval building techniques, learn what keeps buildings standing up, and then build their own cabins to test what they've learned.

KEEP IN MIND The Cité de l'Architecture et du Patrimoine gives guided tours for kids that include hands-on activities (in French, but most guides speak English; tel. 01–58–51–52–00; €8) and for adults (€7). It also organizes special events year-round and offers many longer-term classes.

MAKE THE MOST OF YOUR TIME Near the Palais de Chaillot are other great kid-friendly museums. At Galliria (10 av. Pierre-1er-de-Serbie, tel. 01–56–52–86–00, www.paris.fr), a fashion museum, young fashionistas can learn how to personalize their jeans. The Musée d'Art Moderne de la Ville de Paris (11 av. Président-Wilson, tel. 01–53–67–40–00, www.paris.fr) houses the city's modern-art collection. The Palais de Tokyo, Site de Création Contemporaine (13 av. Président-Wilson, tel. 01–47–23–38–86, www.palaisdetokyo.com) organizes workshops aimed at stimulating kids' creativity.

17 pl. du Trocadéro, 16e. Métro: Trocadéro

 Cité de l'Architecture et du Patrimoine 01-58-51-82-00, www.citechaillot.fr; Musée de la Marine 01-53-65-69-69, www.musee-marine.fr

Cité de l'Architecture et du Patrimoine €7 permanent collection (€10 permanent and temporary collections) ages 18 and up, temporary exhibits extra; Musée de la Marine €7 adults 19 and up

Cité de l'Architecture et du Patrimoine M and W–Su 11–7, Th 11–9; Musée de la Marine M and W–Su 10–6

 6 and up

Full-scale models of facades and other features of some of France's most beautiful buildings from the Middle Ages to the 18th century give you a close-up look at various architectural styles. Kids like the interactive displays that let you put the models into their contexts. The gallery devoted to modern and contemporary architecture contains a re-creation of an apartment designed by the great Le Corbusier for Marseille's Cité Radieuse housing project—it's more than 50 years old yet still contemporary.

Next door, the Musée de la Marine honors France's long history as a sailing nation. Here kids should like the gilded figures that once adorned *La Réale*, a ship in Louis XIV's navy, as well as a collection of sextants and other nautical instruments from the past. Budding sailors can have a great time identifying the models of various vessels, from galleons to aircraft carriers. This museum also gives guided tours and crafts workshops for kids that should delight the younger boat-lovers in your group, and the bookstore sells boat-related toys. All in all, the venerable Palais de Chaillot still has a lot to offer kids and their families.

EATS FOR KIDS **Paul** (61 rue de la Pompe, tel. 01–45–03–55–60) has tasty sandwiches, salads, and desserts. Try **La Matta** (23 rue de l'Annonciation, tel. 01–40–50–04–66) for pasta, pizza, and tiramisu. If you visit the Musée Guimet, don't miss its **in-house café,** which serves delicious dishes representing various Asian cuisines.

PALAIS DE LA DÉCOUVERTE

The sprawling Palais de la Découverte (Palace of Discovery), opened in the 1930s and now updated for the 21st century, contains kid-pleasing hands-on displays illustrating scientific principles. As part of the museum's mission to reach out to young visitors, staff members perform around 40 scientific experiments every day that kids can watch. The *programme de la journée* (day's schedule) posted just inside the entrance to the museum tells you which experiments are scheduled the day you visit.

Among the exhibits, one allows you to make lightning, another to whirl the planets around the sun, another to view the effects of static electricity on your own hair, and still another lets you make a visual display of sounds using an oscilloscope. The École de Rats (Rats' School) is a fascinating demonstration of how animals learn. Acoustics, electromagnetic fields, spectrography, genetics, the workings of a color television, and biochemistry are among the subjects made accessible—and fun—by the museum's creative exhibits. Kids

KEEP IN MIND The Grand Palais east of the Palais de la Découverte and the Petit Palais just beyond it were both built for the Paris world's fair of 1900, and both are still attracting visitors. The Grand Palais (www.grandpalais.fr) hosts major temporary exhibitions. Most of these aren't specifically kid-friendly, but the Petit Palais (av. Winston Churchill, tel. 01–53–43–00–00, www.petitpalais.paris.fr), now the Musée des Beaux-Arts de la Ville de Paris, is a great place for kids to get a quick lesson in art history: it displays art and artifacts from ancient Egypt all the way up to 1900, and there's no entrance fee except for temporary exhibits (T–Su 10–6).

Av. Franklin-Roosevelt, 8e.
Métro: Franklin Roosevelt

 €7 adults 18 and up;
planetarium €3.50 ages
5 and up

 T–Sa 9:30–6, Su 10–7

01–56–43–20–20;
www.palais-decouverte.fr

3 and up

also gravitate to the Pi room, where they may learn that math can actually be interesting, and the Terre et Vie (Earth and Life) room, which focuses on the environment.

The planetarium, which has a 15-meter-high (50-foot) ceiling and seats 200, deserves a visit for its celestial show illustrating the movements of stars and planets. Even kids who don't understand the accompanying French narration can pick out familiar constellations and watch the solar system in action. The museum's popular gallery dedicated to space exploration, sure to please science-fiction lovers, displays a gift to the museum from the United States: a fragment of moon rock brought back by the *Apollo 11* crew in 1969. Like the museum, it's the essence of discovery.

EATS FOR KIDS
The **Jardin du Petit Palais** within the recently restored Petit Palais (av. Winston-Churchill, tel. 01–53–43–00–40) is a light-filled café where you can have snacks or lunch overlooking the garden courtyard; it's planted to look much as it did in 1900. Also consider places to eat along the Champs-Élysées, although they may be expensive.

MAKE THE MOST OF YOUR TIME
The Palais de la Découverte puts on some of Paris's most exciting kid-friendly temporary exhibits and organizes very popular classes for kids 8–12 (in French). In one recent class, kids learned all about DNA; in another, they used real scientific equipment to do experiments in physics and biology. One of this museum's strong points is that even if your kids don't participate in the classes, they are sure to be interested in watching some of the many experiments staff members perform here every day.

PARC ANDRÉ CITROËN

This very modern park covering 14 hectares (about 35 acres) on the banks of the Seine has come full circle. In the early 19th century, the village of Javel stood here, surrounded by a grassy pasture known for its wildflowers. The street near the park that's now called rue des Cévennes used to be called rue des Marguerites (Daisy Street). A big bleach factory was eventually built on part of the pasture (bleach in France is still called *eau de Javel*), and car maker André Citroën constructed a gigantic automobile assembly plant on what remained of the open space. Both factories were torn down to make way for this park, and today it offers many attractions for kids.

Unlike most Parisian parks, this one has plenty of open space with grass for kids to run around on (check out the Sequoia planted near one of the lawns), and they can explore a series of gardens with different themes, including the Jardin Blanc (White Garden), which has all white flowers; the Jardin Noir (Black Garden), containing all dark flowers; the Jardins Seriels (Serial Gardens), with plants that are supposed to evoke the colors of

EATS FOR KIDS **Le Bistro d'André** (232 rue St-Charles, tel. 01–45–57–89–14), an old-fashioned restaurant, specializes in classic dishes—like roast leg of lamb with potatoes or beef with mushroom sauce—at very reasonable prices, and there's a menu for kids.

MAKE THE MOST OF YOUR TIME For a bird's-eye view of the city, take a ride in the park's Eutelsat balloon, billed as the biggest tethered hot-air balloon in the world. It takes you 150 meters (around 450 feet) above the park. The 10-minute rides are given daily year-round from around 9 AM to around 30 minutes before the park closes, but only if the weather cooperates. Call to make sure the balloon is running on the day you visit (tel. 01–44–26–20–00). Weekends €12 adults, €10 kids 12–17, €5 kids 3–11; slightly cheaper weekdays.

six different metals (heavy metal goes green?); and the Jardin en Mouvement (Garden in Movement), where plants and wildflowers (in honor of the park's past) have been left to their own devices. Scattered around these gardens are benches where you can enjoy a quiet break from sightseeing or have a picnic lunch. There's also a labyrinth that kids love to lose you in.

One kid-pleaser is a series of fountains near the Jardin Noir that are run on computer-controlled timers and gush forth in unpredictable ways. Although signs say playing in the fountains is not allowed, guards usually look the other way on hot summer days, when you'll see Parisian kids running around having a great time getting soaked. Whether or not they get wet in the fountains, kids can still work off steam on the climbing equipment, swings, and slides in the play area next to the Jardin Blanc.

KEEP IN MIND A fun way to come to this park from the center of Paris is to travel by boat. Take the Batobus (see Bateaux Parisiens, #65: Make the Most of Your Time) and get off at the Quai André-Citroën stop. Otherwise, from near the Balard métro station you can catch a ride on Paris's newest tramway, which runs along the city's southern edge. You can also combine a trip to this park with a visit to Aquaboulevard (#68).

PARC ASTÉRIX

At this French theme park in a huge forest north of Paris, Astérix and his band of jovial Gauls replace Mickey and his crew. Throughout the park, actors stage performances that almost bring French history to life—though the focus is on fun rather than historical accuracy—and leave kids with a vivid impression of a bunch of rambunctious Gauls making life miserable for the invading Romans. Action-loving kids will find outstanding rides they won't soon forget.

Seven themed areas make up the park: the village of the Gauls, the Roman Empire, ancient Greece, the Middle Ages, the 18th and 19th centuries, the Via Antiqua (highlighting villages featured in the Astérix books), and modern times. Throughout the park, actors perform scenes starring the comic-strip characters every French kid knows: little, clever Astérix (the Gauls' hero); powerful, fat, gluttonous Obélix (whose job is hauling *menhirs*, huge stones the Gauls considered magic) and his tiny dog Idée-Fixe; Panoramix, the Gauls' clever Druid; Assurancetourix, the local (bad) poet; and Abraracourcix, the Gauls' leader, fearless except when he thinks the sky is going to fall on his head.

MAKE THE MOST OF YOUR TIME
By car, take the A1 highway north from Paris to the Parc Astérix exit (around 35 kilometers, or 22 miles; about 45 minutes). By rail, take the RER commuter train, line B, to Charles-de-Gaulle airport, terminal 1, from which you can take a Parc Astérix bus from the airport's Gare Routière, Quai A3 to the park entrance. A combination Parc Astérix–transportation pass, sold at most métro and RER stations, covers transport by RER and bus and park admission. A Parc Astérix shuttle bus leaves from the Carrousel du Louvre's underground bus parking lot at 8:45 AM and departs the park at 6:30 PM.

Near the village of Plailly

 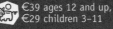 €39 ages 12 and up, €29 children 3–11

08–26–30–10–40; www.parcasterix.com

 In general, Apr–early Nov, daily 10–7; longer hrs in July–Aug, check the Web site (available in English) for exact dates and times

3 and up

Rides suit all tastes and ages, from an old-fashioned merry-go-round to two tall roller coasters: Goudurix (billed as the biggest in Europe) and Tonnerre de Zeus (Zeus's Thunder). Other top picks are the Forêt des Druides (Druids' Forest), where giant trees turn out to be super-high slides, and Éspions de César (Cesar's Spies), which lets kids ride around on pedal-powered chariots and spy on the Romans and the Gauls. Youngsters can join a parade led by Astérix and his men or ride the Serpentin, a low-key roller coaster. The whole family should like the Trace de Hourra, an exciting run on a bobsled track, and the Rue de Paris, where you stroll through medieval Paris and watch craftsmen at work. On hot summer days, ride the Menhir Express (with a 13-meter/43-foot swoop) or the less-scary Le Grand Splatch (The Big Splash) roller coasters; you're guaranteed to get satisfyingly drenched.

EATS FOR KIDS

The park is filled with 40 different snack bars and restaurants, such as **La Halte des Chevaliers** (The Knight's Place). At most restaurants, you can sample Obélix's favorite: wild boar (in pâté or burgers). Several picnic areas are another option.

KEEP IN MIND The Adventures of Astérix is a series of more than 30 French comic books (now in hard-bound versions) that follow the exploits of a band of Gauls as they resist the Roman occupation of their country, often relying on a magic potion that gives them short-term super-human strength. The books have been translated into more than 100 languages (including English) and appeal to all ages: young kids like the fights and simple gags, while older kids and adults appreciate the many puns and allusions, which are especially funny in French. You can find Astérix books in French in most Parisian bookstores.

PARC DE LA VILLETTE

park for the new century, this huge expanse replaced decaying warehouses and slaughterhouses. There are few formal flower gardens here and few lawns you can't walk on. Instead, there are large areas of grass for running around, curving sidewalks (good for rollerblading), bike trails, little bridges crossing a canal, and wonderful gardens and play areas designed to spark kids' imaginations.

The most exciting garden for children, the Jardin du Dragon (Dragon Garden), contains an enormous dragon-shape climbing structure that you can descend via stairs or by a long, long, long curving slide. In the Jardin des Miroirs (Garden of Mirrors), mirrors reflect magically into a densely planted band of trees. The Jardin des Frayeurs Enfantines (Garden of Things that Scare Kids) won't scare kids at all, although its strange deep-jungle noises are fun to hear in the middle of such a big city. The Jardin des Vents et des Dunes (Garden of Wind and Dunes), only for kids under 12 and their parents, has a series of weird humps and mounds that children are supposed to climb on while trying to keep their balance,

MAKE THE MOST OF YOUR TIME

If you decide to take a ride on Paris's canals (see Paris Canal, #8), take the time to visit this park before or after your cruise, which begins or ends in the canal that bisects the park. Kids will need to do some running around before or after spending 2½ hours on a boat.

EATS FOR KIDS There are several snack bars in the park; to find them, look for the knife-and-fork symbol on park maps. **My Boat** (211 av. Jean Jaurès, tel. 01–42–09–26–40), on the western edge of the park, has a wide choice of grilled and steam-cooked dishes (*vapeur* means "steam") that you can enjoy on a lovely terrace overlooking the canal; there's a special kids' menu for €7. For food see also Cité des Sciences et de l'Industrie (#54), Cité de la Musique (#56), and Cité des Enfants (#55).

Main entrance: Place de la Porte de
Pantin, 19e. Métro: Porte-de-Pantin

 Free

Daily 24 hrs

 01–40–03–75–75;
www.lavillette.com

All ages

along with air mattresses, kites, big pieces of stretched canvas that flap in the wind like sails, and other surprising stuff designed to demonstrate the effects of wind and terrain. In the Jardin des Voltiges (Balancing-Act Garden), kids can try climbing walls and maintaining their balance on swirling disks. The Jardin de la Treille is a peaceful retreat with fountains and all kinds of plants growing on trellises.

Special outdoor-oriented workshops for kids are a big draw at the park. Children as young as 2 can participate in one of the many fascinating hour-and-a-half to two-hour workshops. Highlights include a workshop on found objects where kids find shells, seeds, and other natural objects, learn about their origins, and use them to fashion a personalized bracelet. Kids can also sing French *chansons*, learn about aromatic plants and their uses, or discover the secrets of a Persian rug. Older kids can learn to cook Cajun cuisine. There are also ateliers offered for families with kids 7 and older. All are in French and are free with entrance to the park.

KEEP IN MIND For information on the park's current cultural events for kids and families, call or stop by the Folie Information desk at the park entrance facing the Porte–de–Pantin métro stop; it's open daily 8:30–6:30 (tel. 01–40–03–75–75). The Festival du Cinema de Plein Air (tel. 01–40–03–75–75) is a series of free open-air movies shown on a giant screen in the park (July–August, around 10 PM). You can rent lawn chairs and blankets or BYOB (bring your own blanket). There are always some films especially suitable for kids on the program.

PARC GEORGES BRASSENS

You'd never guess that this hilly collection of gardens, kids' play areas, and other attractions surrounding an artificial lake was ever anything except a public park, but two statues of bulls recall the area's former existence as the site of a slaughterhouse. Named for one of France's most popular singer-poets, this park stands out from others in Paris in that its natural elements seem less hemmed in and tamed. Instead of big expanses of gravel with carefully trimmed flower beds along the edges and *pelouse interdite* (keep off the grass) signs everywhere, you'll find a little river running down a hill that kids can jump over and get their feet wet in, a real vineyard whose grapes are harvested and made into wine every year, and a large expanse of grass on which you can actually sit.

Kids like sailing sailboats in the lake, climbing up the belvedere (a little tower in the lake that's reached by a bridge), and riding on the park's vintage merry-go-round. Perhaps the most exciting of all for kids is climbing up and down a steep, rocky cliff that looks like a real mountainside, while their parents watch from a grassy slope across the way.

MAKE THE MOST OF YOUR TIME This park is a short walk from the Marché aux Puces de la Porte de Vanves, a small flea market held on weekends along the avenue Porte de Vanves and side streets. You'll find a lot of junk as well as—if you're lucky— some treasures, from old lace curtains to quirky French kitchen utensils and maybe even toys. If you don't feel like walking, you could take a short ride on Paris's sleek new tram line, the T3, which runs along the city's southern edge and stops near Georges-Brassens park and near the flea market (the Didot stop). Use a métro ticket for your ride.

40 rue des Morillons, 15e. Métro: Porte de Vanves; Tram 3 Georges-Brassens

 Free; some rides charge

 Daily 9–sunset

08–92–68–30–30; www.parisinfo.com or www.paris.fr Mairie de Paris

 All ages

The park's little theater is the site of regular Guignol puppet shows, and the collection of state-of-the-art climbing equipment includes a suspension bridge, little rooms on stilts you climb up to on ladders, and all kinds of jungle gyms. A profusion of flowers supports the park's own bees; honey is made here every year, and classes in beekeeping are given regularly.

Among its innovative attractions, the park contains a fragrant *jardin de senteurs* (garden of scents), with all the plants' names presented on tags in Braille, and there's a kids' play area in the park that's adapted to wheelchairs. Parc Georges Brassens is definitely a people's park.

KEEP IN MIND

Kids can learn all about bees in one of the classes regularly organized in this park by the Société Centrale d'Apiculture (Beekeeping Society, tel. 01–45–42–29–08 for details). If you happen to visit the park on the first Saturday in October, you can buy honey made by the Parc Georges-Brassens' bees.

EATS FOR KIDS Ice cream and drink stands dot the park. **Pâtisserie Loquer** (25 rue des Morillons, tel. 01–45–31–57–07) sells good pastries, quiches, and other quick treats. On a tiny square facing the park, the welcoming Crêperie du Parc (9 pl. Jacques Marette, tel. 01–48–42–97–34) serves dozens of delicious savory and sweet crêpes, usually a winning meal for even the pickiest eaters. For dessert don't miss the house specialty, *caramel au beurre salé maison*, a classic combination of caramel made with salted butter from Normandy and topped with *crème chantilly*.

PARIS À VÉLO C'EST SYMPA

9

Touring Paris by bike can be a wonderful experience, but you have to know what you're doing. With the advent of Vélib' bicycle stands throughout Paris, the city government has installed many more bike lanes—designated by a white drawing of a bicycle on the pavement, these are sometimes just sections of lanes that riders must share with buses and cars. Since Paris drivers, ever in a hurry, sometimes practice the sport called *la chasse aux vélos* (bicycle-hunting), in which the prey is a bike that's taking up space a car would like to occupy, a bike lane shared with cars is not always safe. That said, it *is* possible to bicycle around Paris without harm, and the best way to do it is with a guide.

Paris à Vélo C'est Sympa (Paris by Bike is Great), a user-friendly bike-rental and tour-guide operation, organizes three-hour guided tours of the city for groups of about 10 people (families of fewer than 10 can join a group). Tours in English are available, and you can choose from a wide range of itineraries. Be sure to reserve well in advance, especially if you're planning on renting kids' bikes or touring in English.

EATS FOR KIDS **Pâtisserie Demoulin** (6 bv. Voltaire, tel. 01–47–00–58–20) has a wide choice of irresistible pastries to fuel your ride; try the *Délice* (layers of chocolate, cream filling, and caramelized-almond cake). For food see also Place des Vosges and the Marais (#6), Musée Picasso (#21), Musée Carnavalet (#34), and Rollers-et-Coquillages (#4).

MAKE THE MOST OF YOUR TIME Paris à Vélo rents sturdy four- and five-speed bikes for adults and kids, bike seats, and bicycles built for two. Two Paris companies offer bike rentals, bike tours, and other services exclusively in English: Bike About Tours (tel. 06–18–80–84–92, www.bikeabouttours.com) and Fat Tire Bike Tours (tel. 01–56–58–10–54, www.fattirebiketours.com). Paris Rando Vélo organizes free group rides around Paris on Friday nights and some Sundays (tel. 06–63–71–20–30, www.parisrandovelo.com), and Vélo Electro (tel. 01–42–81–54–68, www.velo-electro.com) rents electric bikes.

22 rue Alphonse-Baudin, 11e.
Métro: St-Sebastien-Froissart

 01–48–87–60–01;
www.parisvelosympa.com

 Tour €34 ages 26 and above;
€28 ages 12–26; €18 under
12; includes guide, bike
rental, and insurance

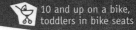 M and W–F 9:30–1 PM and 2–6,
Sa–Su 9–7

10 and up on a bike,
toddlers in bike seats

The Coeur de Paris (Heart of Paris) trip takes you around the historic Marais district, Palais-Royal, and the Île de la Cité; and Paris Insolite focuses on off-the-beaten-track sites like the architect Le Corbusier's house and the Paris Mosque. Paris Nocturne is a tour of the city by night, Paris S'Éveille takes you around the city as it's waking up for the day, and Paris Contrastes explores some bike-friendly spots on the city's northeastern edge. Paris à Vélo organizes tours outside the city, too, such as one to the Château de Versailles. The guides are experts at leading you to out-of-the-way spots like a flower-filled courtyard around a bunch of artists' studios or a park where bikes are allowed on the sidewalks. Paris has about 5,000 streets, and this company knows exactly which ones are right for bikes.

KEEP IN MIND Several streets in Paris are closed to cars on Sundays and some holidays; check the Mairie de Paris's Web site (www.paris.fr, search "velo") for details and to download a *carte des pistes cyclables* (bike-routes map). The Mairie's Vélib' program makes more than 20,000 bikes available in more than 1,400 sites around Paris (tel. 01–30–79–79–30, www.velibparis.fr). Look for the "Vélib'" sign and buy a one-day (€1), one-week (€5), or one-year subscription (€29); there's a €150 deposit. You get a 30-minute free ride and then pay €1 per extra half-hour.

PARIS CANAL

To get far off the beaten tourist track while pleasing boat-loving kids, take a cruise on quiet Canal St-Martin. Head for the Parc de la Villette, on the city's northeastern edge, and hop one of the small tour boats operated by Paris Canal. From here, a leisurely 2½–3-hour cruise travels to the center of Paris through locks, a mile-long tunnel, and even a stretch of the Seine. A guide explains what you're seeing (in French and English), and you get a close-up look at a canal built in the 1820s to bring drinking water to Paris and still navigated by more than 4,000 working barges a year.

Your trip begins at the end of the Canal de l'Ourq; cruises through the wide, placid Bassin de la Villette; and then, just as kids start getting a little bored, enters the Canal St-Martin. Here you pass through the first of five big locks that take this 5-kilometer (3-mile) canal from the level of the Canal de l'Ourq to that of the Seine, your destination. Kids are usually fascinated by the locks, with their huge doors swinging open and shut and the rush of water as the boat rises or sinks. As you cruise between locks you pass through a long, narrow

MAKE THE MOST OF YOUR TIME Another company, Canauxrama (tel. 01–42–39–15–00, www.canauxrama.com), gives cruises from the Bassin de l'Arsenal to the Parc de la Villette (or in the opposite direction in summer), but doesn't take you out on the Seine. The 2½-hour guided cruises leave from the Arsenal at around 9:45 and 2:30; reservations necessary. To prepare for your cruise, you might like to watch a classic French film, *L'Hôtel du Nord* (1938), by Marcel Carné; it's set in the Canal St-Martin neighborhood.

Canal de l'Ourq, next to La Folie des Visites center,
Parc de la Villette, 19e, métro Porte-de-Pantin,
or Quai Anatole France, 7e, métro Solférino

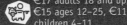
€17 adults 18 and up,
€15 ages 12–25, €11
children 4–11

Late Mar–mid-Nov, daily; depart
Orsay 9:30; depart La Villette 2:30

01–42–40–96–97; www.pariscanal.com

10 and up

park and under picturesque cast-iron footbridges along the picturesque Canal St-Martin. Near the place de la République, the boat enters a dark, mile-long tunnel eerily lit by beams of sunlight coming through air vents that reach to the streets above. You finally emerge into the Bassin d'Arsenal (near the place de la Bastille), a port where many houseboats and small yachts are docked. Then, in an exciting finale after the slow-moving canal, the boat enters the powerful Seine. You cruise past Notre-Dame and under the Pont Neuf to tie up at a dock near the Musée d'Orsay. The whole cruise is a trip back to France's past, to the days before trucks and trains, when most goods were transported on canals like the Canal St-Martin.

EATS FOR KIDS

If the weather cooperates, picnic in the Parc de la Villette before or after your cruise, or sample one of the restaurants nearby. **Cafézoide** (see Cité des Sciences, #54) is a great choice near the place where the boats dock. For food see also Parc de la Villette (#11), Cité des Sciences (#54), Cité des Enfants (#55), and Musée d'Orsay (#27).

KEEP IN MIND Paris Canal also operates cruises in the other direction, from the Musée d'Orsay to the Parc de la Villette, but it's more fun to end with a cruise on the Seine. This is a slow-moving excursion to take with older kids who are really interested in the mechanics of boats and locks (or with babies who'll sleep the whole time). Reservations are required. Occasionally, Paris Canal also offers day-long cruises from Paris into the Marne Valley (€36, lunch not included). The boat docks midtrip near a restaurant, or you can bring a picnic lunch.

PARIS STORY

Want a tour of Paris without ever leaving your seat? You can, at Paris Story, where 21st-century technologies are used in imaginative ways to bring Paris's past and present to life. Paris Story offers three main attractions: the *Paris Story* film, Paris Miniature, and Paris Experience.

The *Paris Story* film, a great introduction to Paris, is a 50-minute movie shown on a giant screen that traces Paris's 2,000-year history, from the time when it was a Gallo-Roman stronghold known as Lutetia to its present-day incarnation. Your guide is none other than Victor Hugo, who shows you how the city grew and changed over the ages. You'll get a look at much more than monuments, since *Paris Story* covers scenes from daily life, fashion and architectural styles, social and economic movements, and more, all presented in an entertaining way using state-of-the-art visual and sound technologies. The lively soundtrack includes all kinds of music, from Saint-Saëns to Edith Piaf. Headphones let

KEEP IN MIND Since Paris Story is indoors, this is a great place to come on a rainy day. You could combine your visit here with a visit to the Musée Grévin (#23), which will also teach your kids about French history in ways they will probably actually enjoy, and to the nearby Opéra de Paris–Garnier (#17).

MAKE THE MOST OF YOUR TIME Paris Story is located in one of the city's top shopping districts. Nearby on boulevard Haussmann you'll find two huge department stores, Printemps (tel. 01–42–82–57–87) and Galeries Lafayette (tel. 01–42–82–34–56), both guaranteed to have something to please anyone in your group. Another possible purchase is the *Paris Story* film on DVD, which you can buy in the Paris Story gift shop or order online at www.paris-laboutique.com. You can also visit two pedestrians-only streets covered with glass roofs and lined with shops, the passage Jouffroy (opened in 1846) and the passage Verdeau, both near the Musée Grévin (#23).

11 bis, rue Scribe, 9e.
Métro: Auber or Opéra

 €10 adults, €6 children 6–17;
€26 for 2 adults and 2 kids 6–17

 Daily 10–7, shows every hr 10–6

 01–42–66–62–06;
www.paris-story.com

 6 and up

you listen in English or any of dozens of other languages. Even people who know Paris well are guaranteed to learn something new about the city.

Paris Miniature, a big favorite among kids, is an interactive model of Paris spread out at table height so you look down on it as though you were flying over the city. All the top monuments, main streets, parks, and other key sites are reproduced in miniature. You can push buttons to light up particular monuments or other features, including the city's fortified walls over the years, or everything dating from a certain time period or built in a particular style. Paris Experience is a display of large plasma screens showing short films on Paris architecture, unusual places, and other subjects; there's even a screen displaying films in 3-D. A highlight here is a film of the Tour Eiffel made by the Lumière brothers way back in 1898.

EATS FOR KIDS Close to Paris Story, both **Galeries Lafayette** (40 bd. Haussmann, tel. 01–42–82–34–56) and **Printemps** (64 bd. Haussmann, tel. 01–42–82–57–87) department stores have several **in-house cafés,** as well as rooftop cafés that are well worth visiting for the spectacular 360-degree views of Paris. Galeries Lafayette is home to one of the largest gourmet food courts in Paris, where you can gather the makings for a luxurious picnic.

PLACE DES VOSGES AND THE MARAIS

The elegant place des Vosges, surrounded by 17th-century buildings in the heart of Paris's historic Marais district, is the city's oldest square, completed in 1612 on a site where King Henri II's Hôtel des Tournelles palace once stood. Originally called the place Royale, the square was renamed to honor the first region to pay taxes to the post-Revolution government. Today, the place des Vosges is a quiet little city park with many attractions for families: sandboxes for toddlers, sidewalks where kids can run around, climbing equipment, swings, and teeter-totters. At number 6 on the place is the Maison de Victor Hugo (tel. 01–42–72–10–16), the writer's former house and now a museum.

The place des Vosges is the perfect place to begin a walking tour of the Marais, one of Paris's most beautiful districts in spite of its name, which means "marsh" (because that's what it was until the 13th century). Elegant town houses (called *hôtels*), built here over the centuries by France's rich and famous, fill the Marais, and you'll find a colorful blend of quiet parks, high-fashion boutiques, chic restaurants, and kosher delis. Walk west on the

EATS FOR KIDS **Ma Bourgogne** (19 pl. des Vosges, tel. 01–42–78–44–64) isn't cheap, but it has good *frites* (fries), classic French, and a great location right on the square. **Le Trumilou** (84 quai de l'Hôtel-de-Ville, tel. 01–42–77–63–98), a budget bistro, is known for French comfort food, like duck with prunes and *crème caramel*. Nearby **Géard Mulot** (6 rue Pas de la Mule, tel. 01–42–78–52–17) is where the locals flock for gastronomic take-out foods and fabulous pastries perfect for a picnic. For food see also Musée de la Magie et des Automates (#32), Musée Picasso (#21), Double Fond (#52), Musée Carnavalet (#34), and Musée d'Art et d'Histoire du Judaïsme (#33).

Pl. des Vosges: rue de Birague and
rue des Francs-Bourgeois, 4e. Métro: St-Paul

 Daily 24 hrs

01–44–54–75–80 Mairie
du 4e Arrondissement

Free

All ages

rue des Francs-Bourgeois (lots of shops) to the rue de Sévigné; turn right and head to the square Léopold-Achille, a lovely little out-of-the-way park with well-maintained climbing equipment and sandboxes. Around the corner on the rue Payenne is another quiet park, the square Georges-Cain. Head south on the rue Pavée (whose name means "paved"; when it was paved in the 14th century, it became one of Paris's first paved streets) and turn right for a stroll down the rue des Rosiers, the heart of Paris's ancient Jewish district. Head south and east to the bustling rue St-Antoine, and then turn right on the rue St-Paul, home of the Musée de la Magie et des Automates (see #32). Go through one of the passageways on your right to the Jardins St-Paul, an ancient courtyard lined with trendy boutiques. Kids can run around while parents window-shop, and you'll get a sense of the Marais's past and present.

KEEP IN MIND

Rue St-Antoine was Paris's top jousting spot in the 14th–16th centuries. King Henri II was killed here in 1559 when his Scots captain-of-the-guards accidentally struck him in the eye during a match (oops). The king died in his palace; the guard was executed.

MAKE THE MOST OF YOUR TIME
The Place de l'Hôtel de Ville (the square in front of Paris's city hall) is full of surprises. From early December to late February, you can join Parisians trying to balance on ice skates in a temporary *patinoire* (ice-skating rink) on the square. In July and August, you can play beach volleyball here, when a nearby stretch of the highway that runs along the Seine is closed to traffic and, along with this square, is turned into Paris–Plage (Paris Beach), complete with sandy beaches, lawns, palm trees, and snacks stands. And it's all just a short walk from the place des Vosges.

PROMENADE PLANTÉE

Also called La Coulée Verte (the Green Course), the Promenade Plantée (Landscaped Trail) is a former train track that's been turned into a beautifully landscaped pathway for pedestrians, bicyclists, skateboarders, and roller skaters. It's one of Paris's top choices for a family stroll, especially since there's no traffic to worry about. The promenade stretches 4½ kilometers (almost 3 miles) from near the place de la Bastille to the edge of the Bois de Vincennes, just outside Paris's eastern limits. Sometimes it hovers high above the street, sometimes it winds through little tunnels, and sometimes it traverses hills, but through the entire length it's dotted with park benches, so parents and tired toddlers can take a break.

Begin near the Bastille, where the old tracks were supported by high brick arches now called the Viaduc des Arts (av. Daumesnil). Within the arches are around 50 crafts shops and art galleries, some with tall windows through which you can watch artisans at work.

KEEP IN MIND

Rollerbladers and cyclists in a hurry can be hazardous to pedestrians on the Promenade Plantée. If you have kids on wheels, make sure they keep to reasonable speeds and stay in designated lanes, and watch out for speedsters if you have toddlers in tow.

MAKE THE MOST OF YOUR TIME
Near the eastern end of the Promenade Plantée is the Palais de la Porte Dorée (293 av. Daumesnil), which houses two kid-friendly venues worth the walk: the new Cité Nationale de L'Histoire de L'Immigration (Immigration Museum/Cultural Center, tel. 01–53–59–58–60, www.histoire-immigration. fr), which focuses on immigrants who have come to France from all over the world, and the Aquarium Tropical (tel. 01–44–74–84–80), home to more than 5,000 aquatic creatures living in state-of-the-art aquariums. Kids of all ages love the sunken crocodile pool.

Entrances from pl. de la Bastille to Bois de Vincennes, incl. 40 av. Daumesnil, 12e. Métro: Bastille

 Free

M–F 8–sundown; Sa–Su 9–sundown; some sections open 24 hrs

 08–92–68–30–30 Office de Tourisme; www.parisinfo.com or www.paris.fr

All ages

Walk up any of the stairs near these shops to reach the promenade. The walkway along this stretch is at just the right height—high enough above the traffic to give you a respite from city noise and yet still allow you to get a good look at the people and shops below.

About halfway between the Viaduc des Arts and the Bois de Vincennes, the walkway crosses the Jardin de Reuilly, a pleasant park with duck ponds and lush green lawns that you can either stop to play in or walk above on an arched footbridge. The walk then cuts through some nondescript modern buildings but soon reaches a stretch of gardens and flower beds. The Promenade ends near the Bois de Vincennes (#62). Strollers can stop anywhere along the way or spend a half day walking the path's full length. Older kids will probably have more fun if they bring wheels (skates, skateboards, or a bike), especially on the promenade's eastern section, which has a designated bike path. No matter how much of the Promenade Plantée you explore, you'll be sure to see Paris from new perspectives.

EATS FOR KIDS Trendy **Le Viaduc Café** (43 av. Daumesnil, tel. 01–44–74–70–70, www.leviaduc-cafe.com) isn't cheap, but their Sunday brunch includes live jazz. The place d'Aligre has a food market every morning except Monday—it's an inexpensive source for picnic goodies. **Moisan** (5 pl. d'Aligre, tel. 01–43–45–46–60) has delicious organic bread. At **A la Petite Fabrique** (12 rue St-Sabin, tel. 01–48–05–82–02) you can sample 40 kinds of chocolate bars and watch them being made. For food see also Rollers-et-Coquillages (#4) and Paris à Vélo C'est Sympa (#9).

ROLLERS-ET-COQUILLAGES

4

Le Friday Night Fever (yes, the French refer to it by this English name) has reached epidemic proportions in Paris. Every Friday night just before 10 PM (if it's not raining), about 10,000 people of all ages gather on Place Raoul-Dautry in front of the Gare Montparnasse for a fast-paced, three-hour, 12- to 15-mile-or-so circuit of the city—on skates. Imagine the population of a whole town, all on skates, careening through the city at night, and you'll understand just how popular skating has become in Paris. If your family includes top-notch skaters, you can certainly participate in this exciting celebration of city skating, but if you'd prefer a more relaxed, family-oriented alternative, you can join the leisurely, free, three-hour Sunday-afternoon skate-ins organized by Rollers-et-Coquillages (Skates and Snail Shells), an association of skating enthusiasts.

The Sunday circuit, like the Friday one, is along a route that changes every week, is organized in advance, and is always traffic-free: the Paris police force blocks off all roads along the routes during the skate-ins so that skaters won't have to contend with cars. Rollers-

MAKE THE MOST OF YOUR TIME Members of the Paris *brigade rollers* (police squad on skates) always accompany the skate-ins, and an ambulance follows just in case. Rent skates at Nomades (37 bd. Bourdon, 4e, tel. 01–44–54–07–44). Helmets, knee and wrist pads, and insurance are recommended. Pari Roller (tel. 01–43–36–89–81, www.pari-roller.com), a nonprofit group, organizes Friday Night Fever and coordinates information on skating in the city. Roller Squad Institute (7 rue Jean-Giorno, 13e, tel. 01–56–61–99–61, www.rsi.asso.fr) rents skates and leads free skating tours for kids 12–15 on Sundays, beginning at 2:45 on the Esplanade des Invalides; reservations advised.

37 bd. Bourdon, 4e. Métro: Bastille

 Free

01–44–54–07–44;
www.rollers-coquillages.org

 Su 2:30–5:30, weather permitting

7 and up

et-Coquillages has designed the Sunday event for beginning skaters, families, and anyone who'd like to visit the city on skates in a low-key way. Show up at the place de la Bastille around 2:15, and you'll usually see hundreds of skaters of all ages, some sporting very expensive outfits and high-tech rollerblades, others in jeans with scuffed skates that have been around a very long time. Everyone is welcome, and the atmosphere is friendly and international. Rollers-et-Coquillages staff lead the way as you skate off through nearby neighborhoods. You might skate up to the Parc de la Villette and back, make a loop toward the Bois de Vincennes, or wind your way through the Marais. The pace is leisurely, and you can choose to drop out of the circuit whenever you like. But wherever you go, you'll see Paris in a unique way, under your own skate-power.

KEEP IN MIND Near the Omnisports sports complex in the Parc de Bercy (see Bercy Village, #64), rollerbladers can practice in the free outdoor Roller-Park. If someone in your family prefers skateboarding to rollerblading, check www.paris-skate-culture.org (in French) for a list of the city's best skateboard sites.

EATS FOR KIDS **Hippopotamus** (1 bd. Beaumarchais, tel. 01–44–61–90–40) is always a kid-pleaser, thanks to burgers and mounds of *frites* (fries). **Dalloyau** (5 bd. Beaumarchais, tel. 01–48–87–89–88) is a sedate pâtisserie/tearoom/take-out shop. At **Le Barrio Latino** (46–48 rue du Faubourg-St-Antoine, tel. 01–55–78–84–75) you can fuel up at the huge buffet brunch (Sundays only, around €29 adults, €16 kids), which includes pastries, eggs, cold meats, smoked salmon, and even a few Tex-Mex treats. Friendly staffers organize special kids' activities. For food see also Place des Vosges and the Marais (#6), Paris à Vélo (#9), and Promenade Plantée (#5).

More postcards are sold of Sacré-Coeur Basilica than of any other Paris site. As Parisian monuments go, though, this gleaming white church perched on a hill is a real newcomer, completed only in 1885. Like the Tour Eiffel and the Centre Pompidou, Sacré-Coeur was reviled when Parisians first saw it, and they still refer to it as a big pastry with whipped cream on top. No matter what you think of its looks, though, you should come here for the views and for a visit to lively Montmartre, a neighborhood that has much to entertain kids.

Begin by taking a ride on the Funiculaire de Montmartre, a cute little funicular train that runs from the place St-Pierre straight uphill to the church. (Use métro tickets for your ride.) As for the basilica itself, kids are often bored by the dim interior, but they get a kick out of climbing up (and up and up, all 270 steps up) to the dome on the roof, where the views of the city are spectacular. Keep an eye on your kids here; some of the guardrails are low.

KEEP IN MIND Legend has it that Montmartre was named for Saint Denis, who was martyred on the *mont* (mountain) by Roman troops (*mont* + *martyr*). It's hard to keep a saint down; as the story goes, Denis picked up his head and walked to what is now Saint Denis Basilica, later the traditional burial place of French kings.

MAKE THE MOST OF YOUR TIME The Musée de Montmartre (12 rue Cortot, tel. 01–46–06–61–11, www.museedemontmartre.fr) takes you back to Montmartre in the 19th century. You'll see furnishings, posters, and a model of the whole neighborhood, all housed in a mansion that was once the home of an actor in Molière's troupe. Le Clos Montmartre (14–18 rue des Saules), the last of the vineyards that once covered this hilly neighborhood, produces around 700 bottles per year and is celebrated at Montmartre's lively annual wine-harvest festival held on the first Saturday in October.

After touring Sacré-Coeur, check out the overwhelmingly touristy but colorful and kid-pleasing place du Tertre, where faux artists fill in the blanks in paint-by-number oeuvres and a few real artists may actually be plying their trade. You can hop on the Petit Train de Montmartre here, a little mock train that makes a circuit through the neighborhood while a loudspeaker broadcasts descriptions of the sights in several languages. You pass the famous Moulin Rouge cabaret, celebrated by Toulouse-Lautrec, and the Moulin de la Galette, one of Montmartre's last two windmills. The nearby Jardin Sauvage (rue St-Vincent, tel. 01–43–28–47–63) is a little garden devoted to Paris's native plant, insect, and other animal life. The garden's enthusiastic guides, most of whom speak English, are glad to answer kids' questions. Take the time to stroll around Montmartre's tiny, steep, twisting streets to get the real flavor of this colorful *quartier*.

EATS FOR KIDS L'Été en Pente Douce (23 rue Muller, tel. 01–42–64–02–67), a friendly bistro, has inventive cuisine—vegetarian lasagna, duck in a salt crust—and a pretty terrace; it gets very crowded at night. **Un Zèbre à Montmartre** (38 rue Lepic, tel. 01–42–23–97–80), a trendy (but budget-priced) restaurant, does a great *croque monsieur* (grilled ham-and-cheese sandwich). Also try the open-air **food market** on the rue Lépic for picnic goods; it's liveliest on weekends. For food see also Halle Saint-Pierre (#47).

SAINTE-CHAPELLE AND THE CONCIÈRGERIE

ithin the sprawling Palais de Justice (Palace of Justice), now the seat of the French legal system, are two of Paris's most famous attractions, Sainte-Chapelle (Holy Chapel) and the Concièrgerie (once the apartments of the powerful royal concièrge). Both are remnants of the days when this ancient palace, then called the Palais-Royal (Royal Palace), was home to the French aristocracy, and both appeal to kids. After experiencing the sublime beauty of Sainte-Chapelle in one wing, you can stroll over to the Concièrgerie in another, to view the gloomy cells where Marie-Antoinette and other aristocrats were imprisoned before they lost their heads on the guillotine during the French Revolution.

Your kids might whine "Not another church!" but they'll probably change their minds after seeing Sainte-Chapelle's wonderful stained-glass windows. This chapel was built in the mid-13th century to house King Louis IX's collection of holy relics, including what he believed was Jesus's crown of thorns, which he had bought for a fortune from the cash-short emperor of Constantinople. Sainte-Chapelle is an upstairs-downstairs chapel. You enter through a

EATS FOR KIDS **Boulangerie Cléret** (11 rue Jean-Lantier, tel. 01–42–33–82–68) has breads, pastries, and light lunches to take out or eat at tiny tables. Lovely place Dauphine is a good place to find a park bench for an impromptu picnic. Charming **La Charlotte de l'Isle** (24 rue St-Louis-en-l'Île, tel. 01–43–54–25–83, Th–Su, 2–8, marionette shows on Wednesdays, call for exact times), is a magical place for kids; like discovering a gingerbread cottage in the city. This tiny tearoom/pastry shop on the Île Saint-Louis focuses on chocolate—all handmade on the premises— and is a mecca for lovers of *chocolat chaud* (hot chocolate), as their silky version is considered by many to be the best in Paris. For food see also Cathédrale de Notre-Dame-de-Paris (#60).

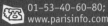
Palais de Justice, 4 bd.
du Palais, 1er. Métro: Cité

01-53-40-60-80;
www.parisinfo.com

Sainte-Chapelle €8 adults 26 and up,
€5 ages 18–25; Concièrgerie €7
adults 26 and up, €4.50 ages 18–25.
Combined entry Sainte-Chapelle and
Concièrgerie €11 adults 26 and up,
€7.50 ages 18–25

Sainte-Chapelle: Mar–Oct, da..
9:30–6; Nov–Feb, daily 9–5;
Concièrgerie: daily, year round,
9:30–6

6 and over

dark but elaborately painted ground-floor chapel (with royal fleurs-de-lys everywhere) used by the king's soldiers, servants, and courtesans. The famous chapel is higher up, by way of a spiral staircase. Once you're here, it's like walking inside a rainbow. Kaleidoscopic colored light surrounds you as you "read" the Old Testament stories created in glass here by unknown artists more than seven centuries ago. Try to come on a sunny day to get the full effect.

When the royal palace was taken over and renamed during the French Revolution, the Concièrgerie was turned into a prison. You can view Marie-Antoinette's cell and her initials carved in a little chapel, see a film on the Concièrgerie's past, and check out a wax museum representing the prison's most famous inmates, including Robespierre. Kids with a taste for gore can visit the Concièrgerie's Salle de Toilette, where you wouldn't want to come for a haircut: people's hair was cut off here just before their executions.

KEEP IN MIND

Free booklets (in French) for kids are provided to help them explore Sainte-Chapelle and the Concièrgerie. Don't miss the gilded clock on the Palais de Justice's northeast corner. It's been keeping time for more than 400 years.

MAKE THE MOST OF YOUR TIME If you have a yen to

see France's legal system in action, you can visit the Palais de Justice's courtrooms (sometimes with trials in progress) and other official areas open to visitors (ages 10 and up, admission free, Monday–Friday 8:30–6). Both the Concièrgerie and Sainte-Chapelle offer guided tours in English; reserve in advance. Concerts are sometimes given in Sainte-Chapelle (tel. 01–53–40–60–80 for concert information). Near the palace, Paris's biggest flower market (pl. Louis-Lépine) becomes a bird market on Sunday mornings; kids love to wander around in it.

Recognized worldwide as a symbol of Paris, the Tour Eiffel (Eiffel Tower) is always a favorite among kids, maybe because it looks like something a clever kid might have designed. When the innovative 320.75-meter (1,052-foot) construction created by Gustave Eiffel began to take form in 1889, marking that year's world's fair, many Parisians—including prominent writers Alexandre Dumas and Guy de Maupassant—objected to what they viewed as a metal monstrosity they hoped would be dismantled as soon as the fair was over. Today, the tower is here to stay, and kids love climbing up and up and up endless stairs through the tower's metal frame to get a spectacular bird's-eye view of the city.

When it was completed, the Tour Eiffel was the tallest construction ever known. Even though it has now been far outdistanced by skyscrapers all over the world, including Paris's Tour Montparnasse, the Tour Eiffel still looks very, very big from the ground, where it stands alone in the big, flat Champ-de-Mars park. Kids are impressed by this monument before they ever get inside it, and they'll get a good look at its base, because you're sure to

KEEP IN MIND To avoid long lines and crowds, buy your ticket in advance online and come early or around sundown, when the light is perfect for spotting the city's monuments. Or come at night when the views are truly magical, especially when the tower's 20,000 lightbulbs shimmer for 10 minutes at the start of each hour, beginning at dusk.

EATS FOR KIDS World-famous restaurateur Alain Ducasse was recently tapped to revamp the tower restaurants, and it shows. The **Buffet** snack bars carry all kinds of nourishing and tasty treats. The **Le 58 Tour Eiffel** (01–76–64–14–64) and **Jules Verne** (01–45–55–61–44) restaurants offer tremendous views, and Le 58 has a good prix-fixe lunch menu. The **Jules Verne** restaurant on level two (with a private elevator) is not geared to kids, but the view is sublime; see www.tour-eiffel.fr to reserve online. Ask for a table by a window. For food see also Hôtel National des Invalides (#46), Musée du Quai Branly (#25), Musée Rodin (#20), and Les Égouts (#37).

Champ-de-Mars, 7e.
Métro: Trocadéro, Bir-Hakeim

01–44–11–23–23;
www.tour-eiffel.fr

Elevator to top €13.10 adults
24 and up, €11.50 ages 12–24,
€9 children 4–11; lower prices
for lower levels; stairs €4.50 ages
24 and up, €4.50 ages 12–24up,
€3 ages 4–11.

Jan–mid-June and Sept–Dec, daily
9:30 AM–11:45 PM; mid-June–Aug,
daily 9 AM–12:45 AM; stairs close earlier

5 and up

spend quite some time in line. On the first level, you'll find Cineiffel, where you can watch a film on the tower's history. This level also has displays on the tower's inner workings and on how it's beautified with 40 tons of paint every few years. At Cineiffel, kids ages 6–12 can pick up a copy of a fun and fact-filled 12-step discovery booklet called Follow Gus, with clues that lead kids through the tower. Along with games and tower-related puzzles, the booklet answers just about any possible question an inquisitive kid might have. There's a gift shop on level two, and at the summit (recommended; spring for the higher admission fee) you can see a re-creation (complete with wax figures) of Eiffel's own office, although the main attraction here is the view of Paris from the observation decks.

You'll see the city spread out before you as if on a 3-D map, and on a clear day you can see for 50 miles. The most stunning view, though, is of the ground far below, seen through the lacy yet massive curlicues and angles of the tower's four supporting columns.

MAKE THE MOST OF YOUR TIME The stairway
between the tower's second (middle) level and the summit is closed to the public (you'll have to take an elevator), but you can still take stairs up to (or, better yet, down from) the tower's first and second levels if your kids insist (though this is not recommended for anyone with vertigo or for very small children). Your kids might like to know that even in the strongest winds, this metal marvel has never moved more than around 4½ inches, but it can become up to 6 inches taller or shorter depending on temperature.

CLASSIC GAMES

"I SEE SOMETHING YOU DON'T SEE AND IT IS BLUE." Stuck for a way to get your youngsters to settle down in a museum? Sit them down on a bench in the middle of a room and play this vintage favorite. The leader gives just one clue—the color—and everybody guesses away.

"I'M GOING TO THE GROCERY STORE . . ." The first player begins, "I'm going to the grocery store and I'm going to buy . . ." and finishes the sentence with the name of an object, found in grocery stores, that begins with the letter "A." The second player repeats what the first player has said, and adds the name of another item that starts with "B." The third player repeats everything that has been said so far and adds something that begins with "C," and so on through the alphabet. Anyone who skips or misremembers an item is out (or decide up front that you'll give hints to all who need 'em). You can modify the theme depending on where you're going that day, as "I'm going to X and I'm going to see . . ."

FAMILY ARK Noah had his ark—here's your chance to build your own. It's easy: Just start naming animals and work your way through the alphabet, from antelope to zebra.

PLAY WHILE YOU WAIT

NOT THE GOOFY GAME Have one child name a category. (Some ideas: first names, last names, animals, countries, friends, feelings, foods, hot or cold things, clothing.) Then take turns naming things that fall into that category. You're out if you name something that doesn't belong in the category—or if you can't think of another item to name. When only one person remains, start again. Choose categories depending on where you're going or where you've been—historic topics if you've seen a historic sight, animal topics before or after the zoo, upside-down things if you've been to the circus, and so on. Make the game harder by choosing category items in A-B-C order.

DRUTHERS How do your kids really feel about things? Just ask. "Would you rather eat worms or hamburgers? Hamburgers or candy?" Choose serious and silly topics—and have fun!

BUILD A STORY "Once upon a time there lived . . ." Finish the sentence and ask the rest of your family, one at a time, to add another sentence or two. If you can, record the narrative—and you can enjoy your creation again and again.

GOOD TIMES GALORE

WIGGLE & GIGGLE Give your kids a chance to stick out their tongues at you. Start by making a face, then have the next person imitate you and add a gesture of his own—snapping fingers, winking, clapping, sneezing, or the like. The next person mimics the first two and adds a third gesture, and so on.

JUNIOR OPERA During a designated period of time, have your kids sing everything they want to say.

THE QUIET GAME Need a good giggle—or a moment of calm to figure out your route? The driver sets a time limit and everybody must be silent. The last person to make a sound wins.

BEST BETS

BEST IN TOWN
Cathédrale de Notre-Dame-de-Paris **60**
Centre National d'Art et de Culture Georges Pompidou **59**
Cité des Enfants **55**
Jardin du Luxembourg **40**
Tour Eiffel **1**

BEST OUTDOORS
Fontainebleau **49**

BEST CULTURAL ACTIVITY
Cité de la Musique **56**

BEST MUSEUM
Musée Carnavalet, Histoire de Paris **34**

WACKIEST
France Miniature **48**

SOMETHING FOR EVERYONE

MANY THANKS

This book is dedicated to my daughter, Inès, without whom I never would have seen a lovely side of Paris meant just for children. I also thank Thomas Ladonne, husband and father par excellence, for his invaluable help on this book and in everything else. Finally, a big thank you to Caroline Trefler, my favorite editor on the planet.

—Jennifer Ditsler-Ladonne

the end